IMMIGRATION ESSAYS

SYBIL BAKER

C&R Press
Conscious & Responsible

For my nephews
Ian, Grant, and Deniz

"The function of freedom is to free someone else."

——— *Toni Morrison*

Printed in the United States of America

First Edition
1 2 3 4 5 6 7 8 9

Cover art: Other Side by Eugenia Loli
Interior design by Victoria Dinning
Exterior design by C&R Press

Library of Congress Cataloging-in-Publication Data

ISBN: 978-1-936196-57-9
LCCN: 1-936196-57-3

C&R Press
Conscious & Responsible
www.crpress.org

For special discounted bulk purchases, please contact:
C&R Press sales@crpress.org

Table of Contents

R and S

For Sybil and Rowan

It must've been blue Lightin' Hopkins that stumbled in,
striking them both like lightening in an Asian minefield

or perhaps it was a late-night late lane change lapse that
just laid there the morning after watching from windows

overcast skies turn into a rainbow. I don't know. R and S
charged and convicted for falling in love with the rapidity

of suitcases. R and S separated by no letters or numbers,
side by side in a line of alphabet consonants. Not a vowel,

not a sound to be made between, yet beautiful in the way
they run together or as if " late for their flight" never did

quite notice that everybody runs away from just as much
as they run towards love. Carry-on bag people, they both

know that a suitcase is the only thing that can comfortably
carry everything. An overhead plane-sized bin says amen

to the randomness of their packing for months in spaces
designed for days. R's mother taught R the safari range

of a rover. S's father taught S to read upside down, letters
after death, revealing a buried treasure of attic sized words.

R was raised behind a gate of privilege though he respected
not the bricks. S, raised suburban wild as rural wild flowers.

South of America Airline lands smoothly in South African.
Baggage claim claims to understand the lack of turbulence.

Neither grew up in slow-poke city, yet race car speed is not
the holy essence, timing is their sacred promise. Schemers

and driftwood daydreamer, re-devisors who wakeup-getup
at the break of sunset red to start not the night but daylight

in the way complete semi-darkness celebrates what it cannot
quite see, the quiet sounds of quiet thunder storms sleeping

quiet under warm blankets of summertime Saturday rain.
On one side of the world, R's father died, buried beautiful

now in stacks of jazz vinyl. The other side, S's mother dares,
still, Virginia in her daughter's daringly keen eyes. Gypsies

are people of no surprise. Kerouac told us that *On the Road*
is a jazzy science. R and S believes in a suitcase god of pace.

It must've been Lightin' Hopkins talking about "Darling,
do you remember me" that they heard that night in Seoul,

Korea. Or maybe Lightin' Boy said, "Take a trip with me"
that night in Seoul, Korea. Nothing but Centerville, big sky,

big eye, Texas blues guitar doing all the sideboard talking
that Van Gogh starry night in Seoul, Korea. It is all there

and here, demilitarized in a zone. We're talking about blue
love, a quiet blue love of boarding passes, updated passport

stamps in blue smoke words, the yellow Latin language of
stage-play-love recited ever so beautifully on the dangerous
balconies and Dover cliffs of life flying nonstop from here
to there. Everywhere stop in Turkey. Istanbul is a bull. So

for now, let us remember cigarette smoke, Napa Valley red
wine talk, a porch perched partially, the shade of a tree while

luggage, itineraries converse weather as two Gypsies part
waters between Johannesburg and Williamsburg, Virginia.

Earl Braggs

Introduction

When I was first awarded a MakeWork Grant in January 2014 to write about Chattanooga's unheard voices, I had planned to interview a few people and write down their stories, which were to be published as small chapbooks. The project quickly became overwhelming—I soon found that there are so many people in Chattanooga whose stories deserve to be told and listened to. Where was I to begin?

Someone suggested I contact Marina Peshterianu, the Associate Director at Bridge Refugee Services. As soon as I emailed her, I realized that I had met her several times socially. We met for coffee, and Marina then put me in touch with refugees who agreed to tell me their stories. I interviewed each of them twice, and as I collected my notes, I struggled with the best way to do justice to their stories by telling them in compelling ways. While I worked on those essays, I also was given contact information for an undocumented young woman from Mexico. After I met her twice, I started writing her story.

By now I was well into my one-year sabbatical at the University of Tennessee at Chattanooga, and the essays had become a bigger and more ambitious project. I began to also write about my own experiences as an expatriate and traveler, incorporating literature and other research into some of the essays.

During this time, Michael Brown was shot in Ferguson, Missouri, a few miles from where I was born. I read about my own family's slave-owning past and Ta-Nehisi Coates' essay on redlining and reparations published in the *The tlantic*. More information was also being published about the "two cities" that made up Chattanooga—one largely white and middle class, the other impoverished, also white but mostly Black. While Chattanooga kept patting itself on the back for its revitalization, it was clear that a large part of the city was not reaping the rewards of this change. I began to think about my own complicity and connections to race, neighborhoods, and gentrification, and how I might begin my own reparations to redress some of the wrongs I have committed.

In February 2015, I continued my sabbatical as a Visiting Professor at Middle East Technical University in North Cyprus. That experience teaching a predominantly Muslim population and my later travels through Turkey and Southeastern Europe allowed me a chance to experience a region right before the migration crisis exploded on the international scene.

When I returned to Chattanooga in the fall of 2015, I wrote new essays about my travels and dramatically revised the essays I'd written. As I wrote those, I began to think about how being married to an immigrant has also informed my worldview in other matters. I knew the essays were still somewhat dry, and my beta readers kept telling me they wanted more of my personal life in the work. I somewhat reluctantly began to put in more of my own experiences in the essays to add more depth to the work.

I also was re-reading and teaching Viktor Shklovsky's *Theory of Prose*, and I was thinking of ways in which photos and footnotes might destabilize and defamiliarize the primary texts. "Reverse Migration," which was published by *The Critical Flame*, is in form my most experimental. Daniel Pritchard, the editor, pointed out the essay was "Sebaldian" (referring to W.G. Sebald, who combined photos and text into genre-bending classics). Intrigued by the comparison, I decided to integrate personal photos into the other essays to continue the "Sebaldian" aesthetic.

As a result, the essays in this collection represent many forms— some are personal essays, and others incorporate research and references to other literature. While they vary in form and style, all of them revisit and return to my own obsessions and questions in this collection: race, immigration, refugees, expatriation, gentrification, family, and the myth of the American Dream.

Writing these essays took many more revisions and much

longer than I'd envisioned. I consider myself a beginner in this genre, and it did take a village (and a lot of patience) to finally produce this collection. I still feel ignorant and confused about the issues I consider here, but am determined to try to keep my heart open to people and experiences that will make me more compassionate to the wider world.

As this book goes to press, the issues I write about seem to be more urgent than ever. On July 15, 2016, almost exactly a year from the shootings at two Army recruitment facilities in Chattanooga, a coup was attempted in Turkey, and the country is now under martial law. My brother and sister-in-law and nephew live in Ankara and I worry for their country's future. Chattanooga still ranks high in income inequality, and the poorer neighborhoods continue to suffer the most crime and benefit from the fewest resources. According to the United Nations, the number of refugees and displaced people fleeing war-torn regions is a record-breaking 65.3 million. On August 7, 2016, *The Chattanooga Times Free Press* reported on Chattanooga Organized for Action's latest report that criticizes the lack of diversity in the nonprofit sector and its consequences on our city's poor.

After I wrote these essays, I asked my friends George and Earl (who I write about in this book) which they preferred me to use in the essays: black, Black, or African American. Earl and George both suggested I use Black. This is the email George wrote in response, which he has given me permission to publish here:

Hey Sybil, I tend to prefer the capitalized Black, because it refers to a people and not a color. Of all the things we have been called, my personal preference is Afro-American. However, I have two children who are people of color. Black does not adequately describe who they are. Tiger Woods tried to describe the race of Asian and African American people as amerasian. It was not successful. The problem we have here Sybil, race is a myth that separates people of the world. There is only one race, it is called the human race. We bought the white man's simple characterization of black, brown, white, yellow and red people a long time ago and now are stuck in this Elementary view of people of the world. The only reason to emphasize one's skin color is to determine who one wants to discriminate against. What would happen if we focused on geography and culture first and let skin color be an afterthought? Finally Sybil, the so-called black people of America are the indigenous people of the Americas including north and south Americas which includes Latin, Central America and the Caribbean. This is obviously a question I have thought about many times. I hope this helps and not complicate matters. I'll look forward to seeing you soon.

Lovepeacehairgrease!

PART I
Visionaries

Schemers

One day, during the seventies when I was around ten, my brothers and I discovered a large house in the middle of a field not far from where we lived. Our family had moved from our starter home in Florissant, Missouri, to a more spacious two-story colonial on the edge of the suburbs of Fairfax, Virginia. Behind our house was a small forest and beyond that a field where we discovered the abandoned house, sprawling and surrounded by dead overgrown grass. We pushed the door open and walked in.

Right away we could see that a family had lived there and had left the house in a hurry. The couches and chairs were still arranged in the living room as if the family were about to watch TV or entertain guests. Upstairs, the bedrooms still had dressers and bedspreads. The windows were framed by gauzy curtains. Clothes were still hanging and folded in closets, and dressers containing bellbottoms and bright scarves and beaded tops with sleeves that flared out. Back downstairs in the family room, we found schoolbooks with homework. But what remains imprinted in my mind were the *Ebony* magazines stacked on the coffee table, waiting to be read.

We were schemers, my husband Rowan and I. I suspect it came from our expatriate lifestyle in Seoul, where we met, and our desire to see a world beyond the one we knew. The more you see of the world, the more precarious it all seems. Rowan—whose family had emigrated from South Africa to Canada, and subsequently, through bad luck and bad decisions, had lost all of their money—felt the precariousness of the world even more deeply than I did. Until I'd moved to South Korea in 1995, my life had been solidly and predictably American white middle class. But, my parents had grown up under the cloud of the Depression, and our family did not waste. My mother reused the brown paper bags my dad carried his lunch in to work. My dad carpeted our house, installed cabinets, and worked on our ever-aging car. We had a garden and canned the tomatoes and beans we didn't eat. Even when he no longer needed to, my dad would make a meal of the samples offered at the grocery store. He went to retirement investment seminars simply for the free steak dinners.

Front of my father's childhood home, Possum Valley, Arkansas

My dad was raised in subsistence-level poverty working on the family's small cotton farm in Possum Valley, Arkansas. While in the Navy in the early fifties, he'd seen dead bodies in the gutters of pre-Maoist China and children begging along the streets of Manila. Traveling through Mongolia, Cambodia, and Indonesia, I'd witnessed countries in extreme poverty and upheaval, countries that had once been empires. One day, perhaps in our lifetime, our civilization, too, would fall. Rowan and I thought that if we planned properly we might be able to survive the collapse.

Often at night in our tiny apartment in Seoul, after a drink or two, we'd come up with some cramped, crazy version of the American Dream: we would make money flipping houses, even though we didn't possess basic handyman skills; we'd quit our jobs and move to Dubai where we'd rake in so much dough we could retire early on an unnamed island; or we'd save just enough money to survive in a hut in some very cheap country until the apocalypse caught up with us. We were working toward an image more than an idea: Rowan and me, framed by two battered suitcases, waving from a car or a boat or a plane whisking us away from the madness of the world. I'd never moved beyond that image, failing to imagine what I'd do once we'd settled into a bamboo hut and battled mosquitoes and strange customs, with no bookstore on the island and no Wi-Fi to download all those books I was finally going to read. Imagining our life beyond the moment we waved goodbye was for later. The important thing was to quit the crazy modern world and its superficial distractions on our own terms.

Some of our schemes had actually worked. In 2007, we bought a house right off the internet. At that time we'd been plotting to work ten more years in Korea and then retire on the nameless island. Then my father, who lived in North Carolina, was diagnosed with terminal cancer. I spent the first months of 2007, my semester break, helping my mom take care of him, driving him to his doctor and chemo appointments. When I saw through my graduate alumni network an advertisement for the last tenure-track-creative-writing-job-in-America-for-someone-who-hadn't-published-a-book at a university six hours from where my parents lived, I applied. I didn't believe in fate, but this job felt like it was meant for me so I could be closer to my mother after my father's imminent death.

As soon as I was offered the position, I learned the university had exactly one remaining forgivable home loan for employees who bought a house in the rapidly gentrifying Martin Luther King neighborhood near campus. Rowan and I were determined to get that loan, so we bought a newish house that looked appealing in the photos we viewed online in Seoul. The owner, a young white guy, had taken a job in North Carolina and was ready to sell. In July 2007, we left my dying father in North Carolina and drove my aunt's trailer packed with family furniture no one else wanted to our new house, opened the door, and walked in for the first time. The house had large windows, wood floors, and a front porch with a view of the mountains. We loved it even more in real life.

For the next seven years we would sit on our porch at night with our neighbors George and Anita and watch people bike past to the convenience store a few blocks from us, then return with a bag of something (beer? milk? potato chips?) propped between the handlebars. Behind the bicyclists was a freight train station, and beyond that was the Chattanooga National Cemetery, where veterans of our many wars were buried. Beyond that was the horizon of Lookout Mountain, where much bigger, older, and more expensive houses offered views of the river and city below. I wondered what those people on the mountain thought, if anything, when they looked down at us, if all we were to them were smudges of dark and light.

Across from our house were the Chattanooga Transportation Authority and a two-story brick building in front of the train tracks. On the second floor of the building were a few apartments. On the first floor of the building a bar opened on weekends. Fridays and Saturdays the empty parking lot of the Transportation Authority filled. From the cars emerged the bar's clientele: older Blacks wearing brimmed hats and dinner jackets and brightly colored dresses and high heels. The bar must have been soundproofed because from our bedroom balcony we only heard a slip of music, mostly soul and R&B, when someone was entering or exiting.

Occasionally at closing time a bit of street drama might erupt—fighting couples, loud drunken conversations, minor disagreements—and Rowan and I would watch from our balcony with bemused interest until the customers disappeared back to their own neighborhoods. In our own way we were just like the people on Lookout Mountain, watching from our lighted perch, safe and removed from the action below.

One late Friday afternoon, after living in our house for about six months, Rowan and I walked over to the bar to introduce ourselves. On the door to the bar was a sign saying people under the age of thirty were not allowed in. Being over thirty, we opened the door.

A barrel-chested man and a woman in tight leather pants, large hoop earrings, and close-cropped white hair were stocking the fridge behind the bar with 40s. The man, named Mike, was the owner of the bar, which for reasons still not clear to me was called My Uncle's Place. When we told him we lived across the street, he invited us to come back that evening or any other time. He told us he wanted his bar to be "international." In our neighborhood, international, I realized, meant Mike was okay with allowing white folks into his Black bar.

When we returned that evening, Mike ran over from around the bar and embraced us, leading us to one of the card tables near the dance floor. Men wore fedoras and porkpie hats and suits accented with brightly colored shirts. The women had done-up hair and sparkly dresses and long fake fingernails that clutched proper pocketbooks. Guys felt sorry for me and asked me to dance. They tried to help me. *Girl, you got to loosen up.* But even though we returned many times, I never could, not the way they wanted me to. I felt too old, too uptight, too self-conscious. Too white.

We had such a good time that night dancing and drinking and talking that we continued to return about once a month. Despite some troubles (parking issues, employees stealing inventory, a shooting by a customer right after closing), the bar remained open and popular until the fall of 2010, when, without fanfare, it did not open one night. For months afterward, cars would slow down by the shutdown bar, not having got the word that it had closed. A year later I ran into Mike at the Bessie Smith Strut, and he told me he'd shut the place down because he was afraid of having a heart attack. Keeping the bar open had been taking a toll on his health.

I wondered what might have happened if Mike had been able to expand and develop the club the way he'd wanted, to make it "international." I wonder what might have happened if he'd been white or been given some kind of support to turn his club into something that thrived. But that was not to be. His dream, in the end, cost too much, emotionally and financially.

After My Uncle's Place closed, Rowan and I started a garden with George and Anita, harvesting tomatoes, cucumbers, hot peppers, and lettuce. We bought silver coins in case the apocalypse happened sooner than we'd planned, which we hid in a shoebox in our attic. Finally, with the forgivable loan forgiven and a substantial down payment from the money we'd saved in Korea, we managed to aggressively pay down our mortgage. Six years after we'd bought it, we owned our house free and clear. Freed up with cash, we started scheming again.

We decided to rent out the MLK house and bought a historic fixer-upper on the other side of campus by the Tennessee River and running trail. For the first six months we lived with construction workers and asbestos and lead paint abatement and ceilings that had fallen in from clogged plumbing. We brushed our teeth in the kitchen sink and showered at the gym. We spent our free time peeling off yellowed daisy-dotted wallpaper I detested and then painting the walls a noncontroversial off-white. A year later, our "new" old house was problematic but livable, and our house in MLK was still being rented out to university students.

But schemers are never satisfied with what they have, and one afternoon, I started surfing Zillow again, and that was when I spotted a boarded-up cottage in MLK a few blocks from a convenience store, within walking distance to campus, going for twenty thousand dollars. From the photos of the house's exterior, it looked redeemable. In our experience, paint jobs and regular lawn maintenance worked wonders. If we bought another property and fixed it up while keeping the MLK rental property and our current house (now increasing in value), we could be like those aspirational real estate types on reality TV.

There'd be some sacrifice. We'd have to sell our silver coins as well as our only car, but we'd get around on foot, take the bus, or ride bikes, just like poor people and hipsters. I showed the listing to Rowan, and we decided to check the house out on our own before calling our realtor.

That afternoon we walked over to our old neighborhood and found the house on a little-used side street. We stood in the middle of the crumbling road, trying to assess not only the house's damage but its possibility for redemption. Empty beer cans and plastic drink bottles pockmarked the yard's waist-high weeds. On the front porch lay an inch-thick sponge mattress covered with a rumpled blanket and tree fallings. That porch, despite its rotting wood and spreading cobwebs, was still someone's sometime shelter. In the back, the house was propped up with stacks of bricks where the foundation had sagged. The roof was missing tiles and sloped awkwardly. The chipped and fading exterior needed several fresh coats of paint. The doors and windows were hidden with splintery cracked boards. But until we could go inside, we wouldn't know whether we could save the house or not.

We walked back to the road and surveyed the house again. We didn't have to rent it out to students. We could turn it into a private club in the spirit of My Uncle's Place, where we'd meet up with our friends and smoke and drink and play whatever music we wanted, without having to deal with the increasing soullessness of the local bar scene. Cell phones and people bothered by secondhand smoke would be banned. We'd have a red neon sign on the door with its name blazing away: RJ's Rock 'n' Roll Bar.

We were discussing if our bar would be a members-only venue, when we heard our names being called from the top of the street. Like an apparition, our friend and former neighbor, George, who had been on his way to the convenience store to buy cigarettes, loped toward us. After we hugged, we told him of our scheme to buy the house in cash and then rent it to students or turn it into a bar for our friends.

George said he was cool with our plans, and that he'd like to do something like that himself, before the "whites bought everything up." Even though Rowan and I were white and had bought a house in his neighborhood that we were now renting out, he felt we were on his side. Just like Mike's "international" was code for "white people," "whites" was code for "gentrifiers." George was a fellow schemer, and we'd spent many nights discussing the buildings we'd buy, the businesses we'd open, the rooms we would fix up. George often talked of the bar he'd run for several years on MLK, The Chameleon, until one night before the millennium he left town for LA, not returning until years later. I imagined that The Chameleon, integrated, with its poetry nights and live jazz, was what Mike had wanted his bar to be, and what RJ's Rock'n'Roll bar could become.

George wished us luck, and we promised to get together soon. Before he made it to the top of the hill, I'd already turned toward the run-down house, wondering if we could make this work.

A few days later, we met our realtor in front of the house. Her seven-month-old son, still sleepy-eyed, was comfortably swaddled at her chest. There was no lockbox, so our realtor called someone to remove the boards that blocked the door. We waited for about ten minutes, but when nobody arrived, we pried the boards back ourselves. We pushed the door open and walked in.

I wondered if this time my scheming had gone too far. Boards blocked the windows, making it hard to see what was in front of me. Someone turned on their cell phone flashlight to illuminate the rotted boards, broken bits of furniture, electric wires snaking Medusa-like from holes in the walls. Whatever had been worth something—appliances, copper wire, fixtures—had long been hauled away.

Just outside on the buckling front porch, the spongy mattress soaked up the late summer sun. I turned back to the blocked front door, ready to walk away, to abandon my ambition to fix this unfixable house.

Rowan and our realtor and her baby swaddled to her chest were already moving toward the kitchen. Maybe the rest of the house wasn't that bad. Maybe we could still turn things around. I took another step forward and waited for my eyes to adjust to a world without light.

Our realtor's son was quiet. Cuddled against his mother, he probably discerned a few intriguing shapes enveloped in a cooling darkness. I felt terrible that her baby was here, afraid that this scene of destruction and desolation would imprint on him in some dark, inexorable way.

We carefully treaded from the living room to the kitchen. Stripped of counters and appliances, it was just a space with falling boards and ripped walls. Perversely, stacked on the floor were piles of sheetrock, harkening to a more optimistic time when someone had started framing the area, perhaps looking to rebuild the house. In that same area someone had started work on a dropped ceiling, a project that seemed to be borderline delusional given the bigger issues of the house.

Past the kitchen was a small bedroom, in which someone (the same person sleeping outside?) had recently been living. The mattress, covered in a few tangled, stained sheets, was surrounded by empty 40s, fast food wrappers, crumpled paper, waxy soft drink cups.

The bathroom floor was unstable, sinking from the falling foundation. A stiff towel was stuffed in the hole where a toilet had been to keep the sewage smells from rising. I circumvented the bathroom and walked into the last room.

————————

The long-abandoned home of my father's family in Possum Valley, Arkansas, with its Depression-era structure, was not any larger than the house I was in at the moment. My father's house was on a cotton farm and had no electricity or plumbing. When I was twelve we returned to the old family home. I remember walking through the spent cotton fields where my father used to watch the sky for planes, pretending he was flying to some unknown state or country. Inside his old house, almost collapsed, the walls were lined with tea-colored flowered wallpaper. The peeled strips looked like baby's curls. I knew the wallpaper's main purpose was to keep the wind out, but even so, I admired the aspirational sophistication of the delicate rose pattern.

There was no aspirational wallpaper in this last room of this empty house, only notes of hopelessness magic-markered on spotted walls in a room littered with broken pieces of things that could never be put back together. I read the messages quickly, and I do not remember the words. I only remember the content: that life had not turned out as planned, and in fact life had taken people to a dark empty room from which they'd never escape. They could have been notes of suicide. They could have been the ramblings of a junkie. The f-word was used like a comma. They were the cries of people who'd reached the end of the line.

It was time for me to go.

As I approached the door to leave the dilapidated house, I heard someone calling to us, as if in some alternate world this was our house and someone had come "visiting." They were father and son, the ones who were supposed to have let us in thirty minutes before. They apologized for being late. The father, in his sixties or seventies, wore a red "I love Jesus" baseball hat, and was earnestly smoking a cigarette, almost purposely blowing clouds toward the baby's placid face. After a while, we figured out he was—or had been—the homeowner.

They were congenial enough, happy to strike up a conversation with strangers, the way Tennesseans are inclined to do. The old man solved one mystery after another about the house. A few years ago he had started fixing it up, but there was only so much an old man could do, he said. The leftover drywall and ceiling were his. He seemed proud of the house, said that a lot could be done with it. He said, compared to others he'd seen, this one was not bad. His son said that this house, along with some other properties (including the one next door, still inhabited, with two churning AC window units on each side, like dark, fixed eyes), had been bought up by a woman in Texas who wanted to sell them to the highest bidder. When they sold, whoever was living in them would be kicked out.

We finished our conversation, and like good Southern hosts, we waved goodbye from the sunken porch, sending father and son on their way.

The Baker Family

In the mornings, when my brothers and I were young in our new suburban neighborhood, we'd wait for my father, in suit and tie, to finish his breakfast so that we could run to the bay window in the living room and wave goodbye to him as he backed out of our driveway, heading to his white-collar job working for a defense contractor. I can see us, three tow-headed kids, hands pressed against the window, sending him off not with fear but with fanfare because we were certain that every evening he would return.

———

One day someone, probably a white person, would buy that house and erase those messages off those walls. That white person was not going to be me.

That fall of 2014, after we gave up our scheme to sell our car to buy that house of despair, I looked up my old childhood house in Florissant, Missouri, a few miles from Ferguson, on Zillow. Built in 1956, the house was just over a decade old when my parents sold it in 1968. Now, in 2014, the listing says, "With a little TLC, this would make a great family home." The house, a 1,200-square-foot ranch home, last sold on December 31, 2012, for $36,098, not much more than that house of despair I'd momentarily dreamed of buying.

I wonder if the inside of my childhood home would look the way I remember it. The narrow hall that led to my bedroom where an evil red clown on the wall threatened me at night. The table where my baby brother peed on me while I watched my father change his diaper. The chair in the kitchen I'd sit in to watch *The Three Stooges* on our tiny black-and-white TV and eat M&Ms from a cup. Until I got my tonsils out when I was four, I was often sick in that house, not allowed to go to church or the grocery store, so my life didn't extend beyond our tiny cul-de-sac of a street. But it was enough. When I was well, the house opened onto a street where everything was possible. I would meet my neighbor friends and we would ride our tricycles and wear plastic jewelry that sparkled and gossip about whatever three-year-olds gossiped about. On the best days my mom would fix me my favorite sandwich, butter and ketchup on white bread, and I'd watch in awe as my five-year-old neighbor rode his banana-seat bike without training wheels down our street.

But the best memory of that time was when in the summer evenings a city truck would spew DDT to kill the mosquitoes, fat and fertile, the clouds thick in the humid air. As our parents watched from their lawns, my neighbor friends and I, all under five years old, chased each other in those silvery puffs, pretending to be lost in the fog or angels floating in heaven.

When I was four, after my tonsils were cut out and I no longer was sick, my dad, an engineer, got a better job with a better home in a better place in Virginia. Our Florissant starter home was temporary, just a step on the ladder to white-collar success. I remember sitting in the station wagon, waving goodbye to that first house. But I wasn't sad; I didn't cry. After all, our new house and yard would be bigger and better. Unlike Rowan, unlike Mike, unlike George, unlike the man with the Jesus hat, unlike the person who had written words of despair on those crumbling bedroom walls, unlike the family who had optimistically stacked their *Ebony* magazines as if they had all the time in the world, unlike Michael Brown, shot a few miles from where I was born, unlike them, this was the America I knew. Like my dad, so far from Possum Valley, I was going somewhere.

I couldn't imagine anyone or anything trying to stop me.

I couldn't imagine not wanting to wave goodbye.

The Adventures of a Fake Immigrant

After scrubbing any traces of my own messy life from the oven and bath-room tiles, I fell asleep on the love seat waiting for the Germans to arrive. It was closer to midnight than not, with stars blinkering the winter sky. Usually at this time of year—early January—the living room where I dozed would be warm from the dying embers of the logs from the fire Rowan had built, but this night all I could do was wrap myself in a blanket, close my eyes, and wait. I wondered if the Germans had been detained by immigration at the Atlanta airport or gotten lost driving to Chattanooga. Earlier that day I'd packed a suitcase with enough clothes to survive seven months, three seasons, and nine countries, a suitcase that was now deposited in a bedroom on the second floor of George and Anita's house in our former neighborhood of Martin Luther King. We were renting a room from them at a very reasonable rate for the next month before I left for Cyprus.

In a month, I was going to start my semester as a visiting professor at a university in Cyprus where I'd continue my sabbatical writing project. Rowan was to follow at the end of April, when he finished teaching at our university in Chattanooga. We planned to spend July traveling around Southeastern Europe, something we'd been looking forward to for the past year. We both loved traveling, especially to places that allowed us see the world differently. For the next six months we were to be, as my father-in-law would say, "untethered." But even though we planned to travel cheaply, we still needed enough cash to pay our mortgage and fund our travels. We decided our best option was to rent out our house.

A few months earlier, in September, shortly after we'd abandoned our scheme to buy a run-down house in our old neighborhood for cash, Rowan learned a visiting professor from Germany was looking for a furnished house to rent for six months starting in January. Our house, a few blocks from campus and near downtown, was perfect for the professor, and we agreed, over an email handshake, to rent the house to him for six months. That we would have to move out of our house while we were still in Chattanooga was a minor issue we assumed would resolve itself.

But as the weeks crept closer to the German family's arrival, Rowan and I still hadn't secured a temporary dwelling. We couldn't find a furnished apartment on a month-to-month lease for less than what we were charging the Germans. Even AirBnB, still a nascent industry in Chattanooga, didn't yield any options. Our friends around town offered us their spare bedrooms, but we were wary of the negative effects our long-term cohabitation might have on our friendships—after all, we were no longer twenty-something vagabonds, but mid-career professionals long settled into routines and patterns.

We were running out of options. Then one evening in late November, after a few drinks in our basement bar, where such decisions are usually made, George insisted we stay with him and Anita. Before we'd bought our current house two years earlier, we'd been neighbors in MLK for seven years. We'd spent a lot of time at their house, eating George's chili or barbeque and greens, sitting on his screened back porch drinking beer stocked in a mini-fridge, working late mornings on a garden we planted and cultivated in the loamy soil of their back yard because the rocky soil of our own yard a few feet away couldn't grow any-thing. We'd partied through Obama's first election there (we were the only whites in the very festive house), gone to parties for visiting writers and aging relatives, celebrated birthdays, and watched movies on their flat-screen TV.

Our weekly rental payment would keep George in smokes, contribute to the eternal upgrades an old house demands, and sponsor an occasional meal out with Anita. We'd be back in our old neighborhood, a place we'd missed with the nostalgic tenderness of an immigrant for her homeland. Only later did

I find out that George got some shit from his male friends for letting a white girl live in his house. After all, a white girl in a Black family's house could only lead to trouble. But George and Anita and Rowan and I had been friends for years. The only trouble we'd gotten into with George in the past was drinking too much and staying up too late. Now we were getting too old for even that.

Close to midnight I woke up to our digital doorbell and the German professor standing on our porch, bleary-eyed and jet-lagged, apologizing for being late. Behind him trailed his wife and three daughters. After giving them a quick tour with promises to help them settle in the next day, Rowan and I drove the mile and a half south to George and Anita's, dragged in the last of our belongings, and settled into the spare bedroom upstairs with its surprisingly comfortable mattress. Home for the next month. That first morning at George and Anita's, I watched the sun rise over Lookout Mountain from our bedroom window—I'd forgotten how orange and pink the sky could be. I looked past the barren backyard, where a future garden promised to grow, over to the yard of our first house, the one we'd bought when we first came to Chattanooga and now rented to strangers. I tried to imagine our mystery tenants witnessing that same sun shining on the industrial railroad tracks, the National Cemetery, and the mountains beyond. Only a mile and a half away, the early morning runners and bicyclists would be fitnessing their way on the Riverwalk that ran in front of the tall hedges of our house the Germans were now occupying.

Being in our old neighborhood in our friend's house didn't make sense exactly, but it felt right, and within a few days, Rowan and I had established our routine. Rowan was up by five each morning, stealthily creaking down the stairs and out the front door into the darkness. He'd drive our car to the gym downtown, where he'd run miles on the treadmill, soak in the sauna, shower, and shave before shacking up in his office for the rest of the day. Although Rowan was definitely the tidier half of our marriage, his office, a glassed-in space in our university's new library, was now cluttered with the accoutrements of a homeless hoarder: my Keurig coffeemaker and boxes of coffee pods, a sleeping pad and bag under his desk, suitcases full of stuff we'd brought from our house that we might or might not use during our displacement, half-open boxes of breakfast bars and other packaged snacks. He'd spend the longer part of most days in that office, drinking cups of coffee from the Keurig pods, sustaining himself with granola bars and peanut-butter-and-jelly sandwiches when he wasn't teaching. Eventually as the sun fell, he'd return to our room at George and Anita's, where he'd do a crossword puzzle or read a book before falling asleep by eight.

I would wake up a little bit later than Rowan, at 6:30 or so, watch the sun rise, and boil water in a kettle we kept in the room for my Starbucks instant coffee. Sometimes I'd hear Anita downstairs getting her mother ready to go to the nursing home where she stayed during the day, then showering and leaving for the community college where Anita was a math professor. George, who stayed up most nights past midnight, was still sleeping when I left the house, gym bag in tow, to shower at the gym on campus.

———

Before I moved from Arlington, Virginia, to Seoul in 1995, I knew a man named Mr. Cho who worked a desk job at the Georgetown Law Library. Although he'd been educated in one of the top universities in Seoul, South Korea, he'd fled a desperately poor and authoritarian Korea in the early 1960s. He and his wife, a nurse, had bought a house in the DC suburbs, then saved to buy a bigger house, which they rented out to diplomats and other rich people. Their own modest house had a tiny old-fashioned black-and-white TV and furniture they never replaced. One time Mr. Cho bought his wife tickets to a movie for her birthday and she yelled at him for being so frivolous. There were never any jewelry and dinners out or other nice things; instead there was the immigrants' focus on saving and generating wealth to pay for their daughters' educations (one went to Harvard, the other to Georgetown) and as security against the unknown. As Mr. Cho often said, "Nobody knows the future." As banal and obvious as the phrase seemed, for the next twenty years I would return to Mr. Cho's statement, sometimes invoking it myself, other times pondering it like a Zen koan.

Our reasons for living out of our car and a boarding house, for not eating in restaurants with our friends or knowing where we'd stay, while not as extreme, had something in common with the immigrants' mentality. Rowan had grown up a rich and privileged white boy in apartheid South Africa. When his family emigrated to Canada, they lost most of their fortune, and eventually scattered. Even after Rowan's mother and brother returned to South Africa, the fractured family never recovered spiritually or financially. The US was the fourth country Rowan had lived in, the fourth country where he had started over. Our friends, comfortable native-born American homeowners all, no doubt thought our chosen untethered way of living out of a suitcase and eating from the trunk of a car was a bit crazy.

And it *was* crazy—from a middle-class American point of view. But Rowan and I had lived in Korea for years, sleeping on a *yo* on the floor of our one-bedroom apartment. We'd lived without an oven and a car, and loved every minute of it. We'd traveled in countries without hot water or electricity, witnessed families for whom living out of a car was a life of privilege. Some of those families were right here in Chattanooga. There was something about our silly scheme that connected us in a small way to those forced to make larger and more significant sacrifices. And, too, there was the adventure of it all.

Rowan also was itching for a change himself—a last chance to play the rambling man, the vagabond, the flaneur. Our month eating sandwiches from the trunk of our car and living out of a bedroom was just a rehearsal for that summer when we'd be doing the same, except by then we'd have backpacks instead of a car trunk to store our peanut butter and jelly.

About once a week we returned to our house to check on the Germans, to help them navigate our Roku streaming player or show them how to use our washer and dryer or to turn off our Wi-Fi. The German professor lamented that on his sabbatical in South Dakota five years earlier, his now-teenage daughters had integrated quickly into American life, but this time they spent most of their time chatting on social media instead of making friends in real life. He was so desperate to force them into the world that he wanted to cut off their Wi-Fi.

When we visited the Germans, unfamiliar shoes of varying colors and sizes were scattered at the back entrance—pink little girls' sneakers, men's running shoes, chunky-heeled boots. The house always carried the heavy, nourishing smell of a roast or a stew. Once, the Germans invited us to a small party in the basement bar of our own house. One of the neighbors, who in an almost miraculous coincidence was from Austria and had a six-year-old bilingual son, was invited. Cans of warm beer sat on the bar. Rowan drank a glass of whisky, and I had a glass of wine. We played a few games of darts before returning to our small room at George's. In a few weeks the Germans were more integrated and engaged with our neighbors than we'd ever been. It was as if we'd never lived there.

After a month at George's we moved out. I flew to Cyprus a few days before Valentine's Day. Rowan found a one-bedroom apartment on AirBnB that he rented for a month at a farm near the Chickamauga Battlefield in Georgia, a forty-minute drive from campus. After that month, Rowan decided to move a bit closer into town, and he tried his luck at a string of dubious extended stay motels. The rooms were sufficient, but the clientele could be rough, so Rowan decided to park our Miata overnight on campus to keep it from being broken into.

While I was comfortably settling into my campus apartment in Cyprus, Rowan's adventure in rootlessness was turning sour.

Although he would lock himself in his hotel room before the sun went down, he couldn't sleep well because of the commotion from drug dealers and prostitutes in adjacent rooms. One night Rowan listened as a pimp fought all night with several female prostitutes. At 3 a.m., Rowan finally peeked from behind his curtain and saw a man, shirtless, with chains around his neck, pacing the hall. As soon as the sun rose and the coast was clear, Rowan left his room, walking three miles past derelict stores and gas stations through dark tunnels and stretches of highway until he reached the Starbucks downtown, which opened at 6 a.m. There he read the paper and prepped for class before walking a few more miles to the gym on campus. He'd work out and shower before his office hours began at nine, even though no students would come to see him.

Months later when Rowan told me about his brush with danger, I of course chastised him, but I was not too surprised. After all, Rowan had survived even more dangerous situations— waking up in the early morning in a township in Johannesburg in a truck he'd fallen asleep in, having a gun pulled on him in an alley in Jamaica, hiking overnight by himself with no protection except a kitchen knife, which he wielded by his tent as he listened to the coyotes howl. Foolish? Lucky? Yes. But I also couldn't help but believe some benevolent spirit was watching out for him. For now.

After bouncing from one dodgy extended-stay hotel to another, Rowan spent the last three weeks renting a room from our friends who lived in a pleasant suburb in Hixson, about twenty minutes from campus. He was a good tenant, leaving while it was still dark in the mornings and not arriving until late in the evenings, his presence ghostlike, almost invisible. Our friends cried when he left, saying he was welcome back any time.

And then, finally at the end of April with our mortgage paid down, cash in the bank, and final grades posted for the semester, Rowan flew to Istanbul, ten pounds heavier than when I'd last seen him in February, the toll of living off takeout and from a car-trunk kitchen visible on his waistline, despite all the walking he'd done. After a long weekend in Istanbul we flew to Cyprus, where he fell in love with the two-bedroom furnished apartment on a campus surrounded by olive groves and blue sky that met the ocean's horizon. Within a few days, we re-established our routines from our house the Germans were still happily renting, routines he'd had to forgo the past four months: buying food and cooking it at home, making coffee in the mornings in a French press, cleaning the house, going on long walks and runs, drinking beer on the balcony. Except here, instead of train tracks and cemeteries, our view was of the vast rust-colored landscape, dotted with shrubs and olive trees and a herd of sheep. On weekends we traveled by bus or a rented car around Cyprus. After a month and a half, we met my family in Marmaris in Turkey, and then after that we flew to Vienna, and by train and bus spent the next month making our way back to Istanbul.

In Budapest we got an email from our German professor. A business professor at our university needed to rent a furnished house for a month, which coincidentally, was the very month-long gap between when the Germans left and we returned. The dates overlapped almost perfectly—we'd only have to stay at a hotel in Chattanooga for a few days. Another month of rent would help pay for the unplanned housing expenses of that summer: a cracked coil in the air conditioner, so that the upstairs where the Germans slept was as sweltering as a shuttered attic, and a leaking roof in the rental house that required major work to fix. What were a few more days in a cheap hotel, after all this? Then in Bucharest, the German emailed us again: somebody working at Volkswagen was looking for a house to rent downtown. The rent he could pay was almost double our mortgage.

In Thessaloniki during the middle of the Greek financial crisis, we discussed renting our house for the next year. We could live in a one bedroom or a studio and then pay our house off in record time, which would enable us to retire early in South Africa or Cyprus, where Rowan had decided his new occupation would be selling fresh-squeezed orange juice from a cart on a beach. Cyprus had the best oranges we'd ever tasted, beyond sweet and juicy, and you could buy a bag of them for a dollar because the oranges were grown in North (Turkish-occupied) Cyprus, which was under a trade embargo. But as the travels wore on and we grew more weary of schlepping backpacks and living off of gyros (the ten pounds Rowan had quickly shed had migrated to me), we decided we wanted to live in our own house again, at least for a while. Instead we planned to finish the basement, with the idea of one day converting it into an apartment we could live in while we rented the rest of the house out.

Mr. Cho, I was pretty sure, would have rented the entire house out and spent the next ten years living in George and Anita's spare bedroom. The immigrant knows it's best to save as much money as possible as insurance against the unknown. I chided myself for being a bit soft. In the end, I was a fake immigrant.

This wandering, these decisions, this returning, these schemes were my luxuries.

The luxury of living out of a backpack because I want to. The luxury of having a home and a job and people I love to return to. The luxury of counting on those things.

In August, after seven adventurous months of sleeping in other beds and other sheets and of other people sleeping in ours, we returned home. On the surface, little had changed with our house—our sofa and dining room table were where we'd left them, our dishes remained stacked and clean in the cupboard, and our repaired air conditioner hummed with expected efficiency. Our bedroom furniture had been rearranged, but Rowan and I decided to keep the bed where the Germans had left it, across from the dresser, allowing more light into the room. Over the next few weeks I found traces of our guests: the business professor's cat's hair stuck in air vents and coating our old velvet chair, a zip hoodie left by one of the teenage girls, and happy butterfly stickers affixed on our windows, hiding behind the drawn blinds. In another corner I found sparkly pink ponytail holders, which I secured in my own thin hair before my morning workouts. Except for these ghostly reminders of the people who'd occupied our house, it was as if we had never left. Erasure, it seemed, was easier than I'd thought.

Soon after we returned, George came over to catch up. On our deck, drinking a few beers as the strivers biked and ran past us on the Riverwalk, we discussed our summers. Then George told us he was going to renovate his basement and rent it out. We admitted we had similar plans.

"I can't let those white guys take over *my* neighborhood," he said, lighting a Parliament. I didn't remind him that not only had the whites taken over his neighborhood, but two of them—Rowan and I—had rented a room in his house. "I got some ideas, and Rowan, my brother, we have got to talk."

For that moment, before a part of MLK became the renamed Innovation District, as if new buildings for white people were an idea whose time had come instead of one as old as the hills, before a few blocks from George's house the high-rise complex for students would be completed, before the coffee shops and retail opened, before we learned that Volkswagen lied about its emissions testing, endangering Chattanooga's own automobile plant, before Germany's open-arms policy of welcoming the Syrian refugees began to falter, before all this and all that would come, with George and Rowan and me on our deck under the same stars shining on those fleeing a world that no longer existed, for that moment, I was happy enough to be tethered to this fragile life of mine, to a future nobody knows.

Fools

January 13, 2010: It was a rare almost-warm day. George, Rowan, and I were celebrating a break in the cold snap with a few drinks on the front porch of our home in the Martin Luther King neighborhood. The day before, an earthquake had decimated Haiti. We argued about Haiti and sacrifice and endless causes. After a few more beers, George and I texted ten dollars to the Red Cross.

George and I agreed that our ten dollars was no sacrifice and meant nothing in the big picture; we did it out of guilt and helplessness.

Rowan called us fools.

The weather by this time was almost not-cold. We watched a few guys from the homeless shelter down the street pedal to the Kanku's gas station a few blocks away.

I said I knew all that and I'd do it again.

"Well, that just makes you even bigger fools," Rowan said.

The night continued and got colder, but we stayed on the front porch and continued to argue about what to do about Haiti. Wasn't some gesture better than none? But what does that ten dollars matter either way in the scheme of things? Wasn't it better to do something in your own neighborhood instead? And on we went.

At half past midnight a guy on a bicycle peddled by, yelling something at us. That wasn't unusual—people often wanted to bum a cigarette or grab a glass of water. Sometimes they just wanted to say hi. Rowan left the porch and walked to the road to talk to the bicycle guy. Rowan dug into his pocket and gave the man some money.

A few minutes later the guy was off again, bicycling toward the gas station. Rowan carried a large cardboard box full of vegetables up to the porch.

The guy had told Rowan he worked at P&P Produce down the street across from the shelter, and the vegetables were leftovers about to go bad. Rowan had bought the box for five dollars.

We went inside where it was warm so we could examine our bounty: two containers of mushrooms with the plastic stretched over, two bags of small carrots, two shrunken cucumbers, a few white potatoes, a large butternut squash, and about thirty sweet potatoes.

Rowan dumped the mushrooms and a bunch of the sweet potatoes straight from the box into a large pot. He rummaged through our cabinet and found three cans of cream of mushroom soup. He poured the gelled mass into the pot and filled the empty cans with water to pour in.

"Shouldn't you cut the mushrooms," I asked.

"You need more water," George said.

"I got it under control."

With a pair of scissors, Rowan cut the mushrooms into irregular chunky bits. He found an onion and chopped it, and then added some garlic, sliced sausage, and Creole seasoning.

By now it was one in the morning and I was ready for bed. I left Rowan and George, who were still watching the soup cook. Just as I was content that five dollars had brought us this provident meal and the stranger on the bicycle some extra cash, I was certain that my ten dollars in Haiti would provide someone with fresh water, a tarp, maybe a bag of rice.

My donation was just a small part of one of the most successful fundraising efforts in history, with the Red Cross raising half a billion dollars. Five years later, we would learn that the donations had little effect. Only six permanent houses had been built. Worse, 85,000 Haitians were still living in crude displacement camps suffering from disease and poverty, still sleeping under tarps, still dreaming of a home. In 2015, Haitians wondered where the money went, and why much of what the Red Cross promised had never materialized.

But that night I did not know those things. I was still a fool who believed a text donation could help someone on the other side of the world. Fools may be gullible and silly and misguided, but they are also dreamers and teachers and truth tellers. It may not be possible to separate one from the other.

In my bed that night the smell of garlic and onions floated upstairs, sweetening the air of my warm, dark room. I heard spoons clanking and explosions of laughter. I pulled the covers tighter and waited for sleep to temporarily take me away from the world below.

Brief Histories

Walnut Street Bridge

I. The Walnut Street Bridge

In 1906, a white lynch mob dragged a Black man, Ed Johnson, who was falsely accused of raping a local white woman, out of his unguarded cell to Chattanooga's Walnut Street Bridge. They beat him and hung him from the bridge. When the noose frayed and broke, he fell, and dozens of citizens shot him more than fifty times just to make sure he was dead.

Because Chattanooga Sheriff Shipp had allowed the mob to break Johnson out of jail and lynch him, Shipp was held in contempt of court. The case, *The United States vs Shipp*, was the only criminal trial ever held by the US Supreme Court. He was tried for contempt of court and found guilty, but only served a few months in federal prison.

II. Eureka Comb Company

By the twentieth century, John Goldsmith Higgins, a former slave, was a respected and successful entrepreneur in Chattanooga, owning and operating a string of successful barbershops catering to wealthy whites. Wanting to leave more of a mark, he developed the Eureka Comb, the first straightening comb

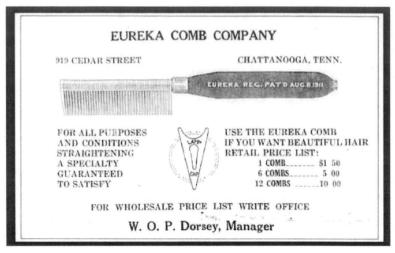

for Black hair, and in 1907, received his first patent for the comb. The comb was an immediate success, and Higgins had to quit his job as a barber and focus on producing and selling the comb. However, according to his granddaughter, Josephine Dorsey Wheeler, Higgins became despondent during World War I because he could no longer obtain the copper and brass he needed, because they were diverted to weapons for the war. Other reports suggest Higgins was worried the US government wanted to take his earnings through overtaxing him. Another article reports Josephine stating that wealthy whites wanted to buy Higgins' patent, which he didn't want to sell. Sliding into depression, in 1919, Higgins killed himself by slitting his neck in front of Josephine.

III. Descendants of the Conley Plantation

With dreadlocks, green eyes, and an Irish last name, George Conley's African and plantation roots are undeniable. Documents show his relatives were slaves at the Conley Homestead plantation in Huntsville, Alabama. In 1898 George's great-grandfather Paschal Conley was a Buffalo Soldier in the Spanish American War. George's father, a paratrooper, fought in the Korean War. He returned to Chattanooga and worked as a "warehouseman"—a deliveryman at a flooring supply company. Even though George's father worked steadily, he was unable to buy a home for thirty years. Eventually in 1974, when George was a sophomore in high school, his father finally bought a house in Hill City with a Veterans Administration (VA) loan.

IV. Dreams and Aspirations

After he graduated from high school, George followed family tradition and enlisted in the Army in 1977, spending time in South Korea as an Army photographer. After he left active duty, he returned to Chattanooga and earned his communications degree at the University of Tennessee at Chattanooga. While at UTC, George met Anita Polk, daughter of Eveline Dorsey Polk, Josephine's younger sister.

In the early nineties, George was one of the few local Blacks hired by the Tennessee Aquarium as membership director. He and Anita had two children and decided they should move from their comfortable suburban home in Brainerd to a house he'd fallen in love with in the Martin Luther King neighborhood. At the time MLK was considered by white people as the inner city, a neighborhood known more for its drugs, prostitution, and violence than as a place of a vibrant Black culture or encroaching gentrification. They started a neighborhood association, encouraging their neighbors to help in a major cleanup, and slowly, through time and effort, the neighborhood started changing.

George and Anita have done relatively well in Chattanooga. Dr. Anita Polk-Conley is a tenured professor of math at Chattanooga State Community College. After leaving the Aquarium, George opened a bar called The Chameleon, the first bar in Chattanooga to draw a racially mixed crowd. After The Chameleon closed, George returned to school and received his Masters Degree in English, focusing on poetry. Now in their spare time they run Eureka Press. Their first publication was *Eureka! He Invented It: The Eureka Straightening Comb* by Josephine Dorsey Wheeler.

After reading the book of a man's thwarted genius, one can't help but wonder, what would have happened if Higgins had been white?

V. The Chattanooga Way

Chattanooga's branding as a cosmopolitan city goes back to right after the Civil War when it advertised in Northern newspapers, asking carpetbaggers to move there, assuring them the city had cheap labor and resources.

For the first half of the twentieth century, Chattanooga was known as the Dynamo of Dixie, home to the "Chattanooga Choo-Choo," made famous by Glenn Miller and his band in 1941. However, as Dr. Ken Chilton discusses in his report for the NAACP, in Chattanooga many of the historically Black neighborhoods do not fit in with Chattanooga's rags-to-riches narrative. Chilton's report includes a map from the Homeowners Loan Corporation from 1939 showing "redlining," or the practice of labeling certain areas as investment risks.

Those redlined areas, predominantly Black neighborhoods, did not have the opportunities for reinvestment and growth that other neighborhoods did. And as a result, many Blacks in Chattanooga have been disadvantaged in ways that still affect them today.

With the decline of the railroad and manufacturing, the Dynamo of Dixie was going bust for both whites and Blacks. The downtown was shut down at night, and Chattanoogans love to recall their lowest moment, when in 1969 Walter Cronkite announced that Chattanooga was America's dirtiest city. Through the sixties, East Ninth Street, known as the Big Nine, thrived with black businesses and clubs, with the Martin Hotel hosting acts like Lena Horne, Cab Calloway, Fats Domino, and Nat King Cole. But, as Chattanooga desegregated and blue-collar jobs disappeared, East Ninth Street began to decline in population and prosperity. In 1980, after protests over a Ku Klux Klan shooting of four Black women on the Big Nine, the street was renamed East Martin Luther King Boulevard.

As Courtney Knapp writes in her absorbing and highly readable PhD dissertation, *Planners as Supporters and Enablers of Diasporic Placemaking: Lessons from Chattanooga, Tennessee*, "the economic decline of the Big Nine was symptomatic of the historical and systematic neglect of Chattanooga's Black communities by the local white-controlled and economic power structures. To this end, the roles of professional planners and elected public officials in coordinating uneven geographic development across the city must also be acknowledged and understood."

The city's comeback and downtown revitalization effort would begin in 1992 with the opening of the Tennessee Aquarium. The public and private sectors worked together to turn Chattanooga around. This type of problem-solving through public-private partnerships became known as the Chattanooga Way. These efforts have continued with more downtown development, so that now at night restaurants and bars downtown and on the Southside are full of locals and tourists. This development has been important to Chattanooga's comeback—very few other American cities have been able to reverse their decline the way Chattanooga has.

Now nicknamed the Scenic City, Chattanooga has a thriving arts, music, and outdoor scene, and continues to garner national acclaim. Thanks to its high-speed internet, Chattanooga's latest moniker is Gig City, attracting startups and other entrepreneurial adventurists to its newly named Innovation District, which edges the Martin Luther King neighborhood and downtown. Some of the historically Black neighborhoods such as Hill City (now the North Shore) and the Southside have been rapidly gentrified and are now predominantly white. Other neighborhoods, such as Alton Park and East Chattanooga, continue to be mired in poverty and are predominantly Black. A 2014 *New York Times* article states that 27 percent of Chattanooga's residents live below the poverty line and that Chattanooga ranks twelfth in the nation in income inequality. In addition, Chattanooga has the seventh highest rate of rent increases in the nation, leaving many residents unable to afford housing.

In a recent Chattanooga Lending and Banking analysis by the National Community Reinvestment Commission, Chattanooga's whites had a 64 percent approval rate for loans, while Blacks had 50 percent approval rate for loans from local banks, with "whites receiving 107% of loans, and blacks only 36% of loans when their proportion of population is considered." In addition, the analysis also shows that there are few bank branches in black communities, because they are clustered around predominantly white neighborhoods.

Chattanoogans like to think of their town as special. In 2015, for the second time, in a popular online vote, Chattanooga won the Best Town Ever designation from *Outdoor* magazine. It has garnered positive press in many publications in regard to its gig connectivity, music scene, outdoor activities, and support for the arts, as well as its natural beauty. All of these, plus the city's can-do spirit, do indeed show why many people believe that there is something special about Chattanooga. However, in the October 2015 *Nonprofit Quarterly*, Rick Cohen writes,

> but what is not special, but rather entirely too common, is the deepening of income and racial inequities in the midst of metropolitan progress. That part of the Chattanooga story is not to be celebrated, but will require foundations like Lyndhurst to redouble their efforts to identify and invest "in initiatives, institutions, people and programs that contribute to the long-term livability and resilience of the greater Chattanooga region," as the mission of Lyndhurst reads, but aiming toward the uplift and advancement rather than gentrification and displacement of the city's working class and poor.

VI. The Case for Reparations in Chattanooga

In his 2014 article for *The Atlantic*, "The Case for Reparations," Ta-Nehisi Coates chronicles the economic devastation done to Blacks not just through slavery but also through the Jim Crow and racist housing policies that continue to this day. During every session in Congress, representative John Conyers introduces Bill

On the back of a sign from Chattanooga's Innovation District

HR40 to study the possibility of reparations. Yet every year the bill does not make it to the House floor even for a vote.

Reparations in the United States are not without precedent. In 1980, after requests for redress from Japanese Americans, Congress established a commission to study the matter of restitution to the 110,000 Japanese Americans placed in internment camps in the US during World War II. In 1988, President Reagan signed the Civil Liberties Act, which issued a formal apology and gave 20,000 dollars in financial redress to each of the surviving Japanese Americans who been interned.

Even if Congress can't agree to study the possibility of reparations to Blacks, Chattanooga can. It's well-documented that racist policies have adversely affected Chattanooga's Black communities. In March 2016, the *Chattanooga Times Free Press* published a series of articles called the Poverty Puzzle.

Using anonymous tax records to map economic mobility across the U.S., a Harvard University study found that a whopping 91 percent of all U.S. counties did a better job than Hamilton County in creating paths to high earnings for children born at the bottom of the income scale. The study found the differences may lie in five measures: segregation, inequality, schools, social capital and family structure.

Across the Southeast, families are caught in an economic trap they can't escape, and Chattanooga now finds itself at a turning point. Do we gloss over our toxic secret? Or do we prove, as we have before, that nothing is impossible when a divided city truly unites?

When a divided city like Chattanooga unites, it can address problems that might seem insurmountable. One step could begin with examining the repercussions of redlining and other housing inequities that have prevented those living in the city's redlined neighborhoods from participating in and benefiting from Chattanooga's renaissance.

In terms of addressing the redlining and housing inequities, several policies have proven successful in other cites and would not be hard to implement. Currently, the city provides housing developers tax rebates in a Payment in Lieu of Taxes (PILOT) program. Developers set aside 20 percent of their units, charging rent 20 percent below the regular price to those who make 80 percent or less of the average salary. However, in a city where the average Black family makes less than 27,000 dollars a year, these units are still not affordable, especially with the rapidly increasing rents. A similar PILOT housing program in Memphis that allows 50 percent rental reduction would be of more benefit to Chattanoogans. Also, Chattanooga could establish an affordable housing trust fund paid for by hotel taxes, giving loans to finance affordable housing. Another option is establishing Community Land Trusts. Giving grants to women and minorities to start their own businesses would be a small way to offset the grants given to big corporations like Volkswagen. On a positive note, in 2016, Chattanooga's Mayor Berke pledged six million dollars for a new recreation center in Avondale. And in July 2016, the *Times Free Press* reported that "the city and county will only consider payment in lieu of tax (PILOT) agreements for housing developments with a much higher affordability requirement than ever before," suggesting that the administration is beginning to acknowledge the city's housing crisis.

VII. As of This Writing (August 2016)

Near the Walnut Street Bridge at Ross' Landing is a tribute to the seven tribes sent away on the Trail of Tears, called The Passage. It's a water walkway and pedestrian bridge linking downtown to the riverfront, and is known for its emotional and aesthetic reminder of an important but sad time in our history, when more than four thousand Cherokees died on the way.

On the south side of the bridge are two plaques with the names of Ed Johnson and Alfred Blount, who were both lynched there. Yet the plaques have no dates nor explanations tied to the names. Any tourist or Chattanoogan would walk by those innocuous markers and not know their significance.

As of this writing, a larger marker to commemorate the lynchings on the Walnut Street Bridge does not yet exist. As of this writing, Chattanooga is still one of the top American cities in income inequality. As of this writing, there has still been no discussion about the case for reparations.

VIII. The History of the Baker Family

According to *The History of the Baker Family*, written and published by my dad's sister, Helen Baker White, the Bakers arrived from England and settled in Midway, Georgia, in the early 1700s. My great-great-grandfather Joseph McRobert Baker was a gentleman poet, state senator, newspaper writer, preacher, and slave owner who enlisted in the cavalry when the Civil War broke out.

Joseph McRobert Baker's last existing writing, "A Reminiscence," was written not long before he died from pneumonia in 1863. This short piece is told in first person of a man, delirious, in a Georgia hospital. The narrator hears a man next to him crying out for his beloved, Mary. At the end of the piece, the narrator writes:

> In the dim, grey twilight of a cheerless winter morning, I am suddenly aroused by the shuffling of feet along the passage. Two negro nurses, bearing on a stretcher the dead body of some poor soldier, pass along in the oft-frequented way to the "dead house," in the back-yard of the hospital.

The dead soldier, who is carried by the Black nurses he was fighting to keep enslaved, spent his last moments alone and crying for Mary to come to him. The Baker family loves this piece, but only now, after many times reading this short essay, do I think to ask, who were the "negro nurses"? Why were they working in a Confederate hospital? And did these Confederate soldiers, fighting to keep the Black nurses enslaved, understand they had been and were dependent on enslaved Africans for their own survival?

IX. The Other Jeff Davis

After the Civil War, my great-grandfather Joseph Paschal (JP) Baker lived in Georgia, poor and in an unhappy marriage. He divorced his first wife in semisecrecy, fled Georgia, and resettled in Possum Valley, Arkansas. There he married again and had eleven children who helped him on their subsistence-level cotton farm. During the time JP was in Possum Valley, Jeff Davis was Governor of Arkansas. Although no relation, Jeff Davis did not quell rumors that he was related to Jefferson Davis, the former President of the Confederacy. In 1905, when President Roosevelt came to visit, Jeff Davis made a speech in favor of lynching.

Never passionate about his farming, JP Baker seemed to prefer his duties as a pastor, a teacher, and a postmaster. And yet, as my dad often noted, for someone so interested in education, none of his eleven children, including my grandfather Elza D. Baker, whose formal education ended in the eighth grade, finished high school.

On January 3, 1913, Jeff Davis died.

In 1914, World War I broke out, and Elza Baker, an army volunteer, was stationed in Chattanooga. After the war he returned to Possum Valley, where he married and raised five children, working his own farm.

X. The History of My Father

My father, Calvin Baker, born in 1931, the middle of the five children, grew up on that cotton farm, but always dreamed of leaving. While his father offered Calvin some of his own land to farm after he graduated from high school at sixteen, his mother encouraged him to leave for larger things. Unable to afford college, Calvin joined the Navy, which enabled him to see much of Asia, igniting his life-long passion for travel.

A Korean War veteran, my father returned to Arkansas after his tour of duty and earned his engineering degree on the GI Bill. He worked as an engineer, married my mother, and raised three children in a house in Fairfax, Virginia. He retired at sixty-two with a pension from the company he'd worked thirty years for, and moved into a house with five acres in my mother's hometown of Clemmons, North Carolina. When he died at seventy-six, he'd lived the American Dream in terms of housing, education, and economic mobility.

After my father died in 2007, I found a slim hardback book titled "Memorial Addresses on the Life and Character of Jeff Davis." Inside, the book is inscribed "In Memoriam Presented to Eld J.P. Baker by The Family of Jeff Davis, 7/7/[19]13." On another page is my father's name written in cursive crossed out, and above that his younger brother Stanley's name is also crossed out. My father must have reclaimed the book. His name is written in careful young-looking cursive: Calvin Linton Baker's Book of Jeff Davis (with Jeff Davis' name triple underlined). My father never mentioned the book to me, but he saved it for reasons I may never know. For now, I too hold onto this book for reasons I'm unsure of, for the book is a reminder of our family's benefit from and acceptance of slavery and its legacy. It is also a cherished memento of my father.

Jeff Davis Memorial Addresses

XI. Mixed Blessings

In 2007, when Rowan and I moved to Chattanooga from South Korea, we'd saved enough money for a large down payment on a house. UTC and the city had developed some grants for artists and educators to buy a house in the Martin Luther King neighborhood, which we qualified for. In front of our house, which we bought from a white guy who had relocated to North Carolina, was the railroad tracks, and beyond that was the Chattanooga National Cemetery, and beyond that was the horizon of Lookout Mountain, memorialized in Dr. Martin Luther King's famous "I Have a Dream" speech: "Let Freedom Ring from Lookout Mountain of Tennessee." Chattanooga Organized for Action's board member, Jefferson Hodge, is not the first to point out that "on that mountaintop the all-white residents make 10 times the yearly income of the all-black residents of Alton Park below. $120,000 a year for white residents contrasted to $12,000 for black residents."

Like my father, who benefited from the GI bill and the other government post-war policies, I am someone who has benefited from Chattanooga's policies. As an artist and teacher, I received forgivable loans to move into a neighborhood that was trying to gentrify. And this very book of essays was funded by a MakeWork Grant to write about Chattanooga's unheard voices, a task so overwhelming that I narrowed the focus to the essays you read here. Although we lost our land and wealth, my family's legacy of slave owning has never been reckoned with: my great-grandfather was allowed to start over without fear of ruin. He, in fact, had Jeff Davis's blessing.

XII. Ed Johnson's Grave

It's just a few miles from my house, past the road formally known as the Trail of Tears, down Third Street, past Erlanger hospital, through the well-kept older homes of Glenwood until I get back toward Shallowford Road. I'm past Avondale, a historically Black community, and Ridgedale, a mostly white suburb. At the edge of this neighborhood is Pleasant Gardens Cemetery, an old Black cemetery that is neither pleasant nor a garden. There's a gravel parking space for a few cars across from neat, middle-class homes. No one stops me as I walk past the chain into the cemetery. There are no signs of where to go or what paths to follow, so I wander the grounds for a while. Luckily, I find it, without a placard or notices like those on Missionary Ridge: a grave marker for Ed Johnson. It sits humbly past the main part of the cemetery, in a tiny clearing with a few other tombstones. But the gravestone is there, and on it are Johnson's last words "God Bless You All. I am an Innocent Man."

As I left the cemetery, an older man approached me from one of the paths. He asked me if I saw the eagle soaring above earlier, its white throat clotted red from a possum it had killed. I told him I didn't see it.

I was too busy digging for all those hidden histories still waiting to be found.

Still waiting to be told.

Ed Johnson's Tombstone

Excavations

My husband Rowan was tearing down the last board from the dilapidated outside stairs of our house when two women from the Chattanooga Historic Zoning Commission (CHZC) appeared, informing him he had to stop. Did we know our house was part of the Battery Place Historic District? No. And did we know that we needed permission from the CHZC to tear down and build structures on our property? We did not. We did not know that in memory of the Civil War and its historic role as a site for artillery placements, our neighborhood (originally called Battery McAloon) was eventually renamed Battery Place. We did not know that for these reasons, Rowan could not tear down rotting stairs without the CHZC's formal permission.

Our house, built in 1927 and owned by the same family, empty and on the market for several years, was to be sold "as is." "As is" meant layers of grimy sixties asbestos-laced linoleum in the kitchen and bathrooms. "As is" meant faded wallpaper lining the walls of the entire downstairs. It meant unplugged and unused air conditioning units stuck in the windows. "As is" meant dodgy plumbing and rickety outdoor stairs coated in peeling gray paint. Those stairs led to what had once been a screened porch, but was now a covered room with glued-on grass-green carpet hiding more crumbling asbestos tile. "As is" meant faux Victorian lighting fixtures and blinds and shutters that were yellowed and permanently dust-encrusted. The house reminded me of Miss Havisham's cobweb-filled mansion in *Great Expectations*. But more than anything, this old house with its white siding and darkened hardwood floors reminded me of a Colonial house from my childhood—columned and stately. We'd pass by the house every morning and afternoon on our bus route, and I imagined the inside promised wood floors and chimneys and secret spaces. One girl about my age would be waiting for the bus at the end of her driveway.

I envied the Gothic possibilities of her life—I imagined she was an orphan who lived with her grandmother. In the books I'd read, orphans were visited by angels and fairies who opened doors to other worlds.

Besides echoing the romance of my childhood, there was another, different appeal to our historic house: the fully functioning seventies-style bar in the basement—something Rowan had always wanted. Also, I'd heard that for a period around the turn of the millennium, that basement bar was home to wild parties connected to our university's writing conference that I helped direct. Apparently prominent visiting writers and locals drank, danced, and smoked there for years. Our basement bar had as much writer mojo as an old café in Paris. Our house had possibilities.

Like Emily Dickinson, I wanted to dwell in possibility. I wanted

A fairer House than Prose –
More numerous of Windows –
Superior – for Doors –

Of course, the two women from CHZC didn't care about my dreams or Emily's superior windows. They didn't care that Rowan was tearing down those rotted, splitting steps because we were planning on replacing them with a nice sturdy deck instead. These women were not here to dwell in possibility or nostalgia. They were here to do their job, and it was their job to monitor any building violations.

They issued a Stop Work notice on the spot.

Rowan "Stopped Work" and started drinking. He spent the rest of the evening in our basement bar listening to country singers and their pain.

A few days later I went to the CHZC office, paid for permits, and applied for approval to build a deck. A month after the Stop Work notice, the housing board gave us permission to build a deck to replace the stairs Rowan had torn down. We also added French doors to the basement bar entrance and a wooden gate.

We spent hours each day scrubbing floors, peeling wallpaper, and painting, determined to erase Miss Havisham's dust and doilies and replace them with our own vision of the world. But the relics of the past did not let go so easily. At night we'd hear creaks and moans, sounds we weren't used to, sounds we imagined were of waking ghosts. One of the plumbing pipes cracked, dumping water into the basement. Another night, the bathroom sink on the second floor seeped water through to the first floor, and the sodden ceilings crashed and crumbled to the ground. Sometimes I wondered if the family who had lived in the house for so long were crying because they didn't want to go.

Confederate Cemetary

We began to feel the house was haunted, and not just with the ghosts of the family who had lived there for eighty years. Not too surprising, given when and where the house was built, that we were surrounded by ghosts.

Ghosts like the Civil War soldiers who had walked on our lawn—some of them buried in the Confederate Cemetery a block from our house on the Citico estate and farm owned by the Gardenhire family. They sold the land for one dollar with the provision that the property be used as a Confederate cemetery. A few blocks from our house along the Riverwalk is our university football practice field, which used to be the holding pen for Cherokees before they began a forced migration west known as the Trail of Tears.

A mile farther past the old holding pen is the Native American Citico site, a large ceremonial village that had thrived in the fourteenth century. Most of the Citico village was used for dirt fill for building Riverview Drive in 1914, but a few of the burial mounds remain.

If there is a house that should be haunted by history, by wrongs and rights, by families gathered and dispersed, it is ours.

What if Rowan hadn't stopped digging?

What if, instead of acquiescing to the women representing the CHZC, I had joined Rowan and planted my hands in the soil?

Toward the end of *Great Expectations*, Miss Havisham, who has thwarted her adopted daughter's relationship with Pip, repents. Her last words, spoken in a delirium, speak to her desire to be exonerated. "Take the pencil and write under my name, 'I forgive her!'"

What if someone in the future finds my name, my books buried here? Will the ghosts forgive me?

If I dig here, what will I find?

A lost doll, a jar of moonshine, a fragment of a teacup.

Buttons torn from uniforms, a belt buckle, bullet shells, a drinking cup, a short sword, a musket, a revolver, a lover's ribbon, a locket.

Pottery, beads, clothes, and pans too heavy for the Cherokees to carry to Oklahoma.

Bones: knee, hip, ankle, thumb, shards of the Citicos' elbows.

Stone tools, copperhead pieces, conch shells.

Before the Cherokees there were the Creek and Euchee. Bone fragments.

Earring-bone instruments, flint knives, pipes representing birds. A child's rattle made of tortoise shell with pebbles inside.

Four hundred and forty-six million years before beings resembling humans walked the earth, there were fossils here, preserved by volcanic ash, along the riverbed.

Shells.

Coral.

Prehistoric jawless fish. Placoderms. Acanthodians.

Dig and dig until we find all that will haunt us.

And all that will haunt others.

Dig until we discover all that we have been.

And will become.

Dig with our narrow hands.

So we can dream of dwelling in the house of the forgiven.

Landings

View from Missionary Ridge

I. Departures

Earl was here first. Cherokee blood from both sides, some Iroquois, too, he'd heard. People tell him they can see the Indian part of him in his cheeks, high and broad, almost Asian, and in the almond shape of his eyes. Other people who claim to know such things say the rest of him must have come from Senegal or Ghana.

Until he was five, Earl lived with his paternal grandmother, the only Blacks in a small community outside Wilmington, North Carolina. He remembers tagging along with his grandmother to the white houses in the neighborhood. She was paid to do light cleaning. Mostly, though, Earl remembers his grandmother watching soap operas with the lonely white housewives who must have needed company even more than a clean house.

After he graduated from high school, Earl joined the military, got his BA on the GI bill, and later earned an MFA in poetry. He published some poems, got a tenure-track job in Chattanooga in the early nineties, and began publishing the first of many books of poetry. A few years later, he met Natalie, an immigrant from the Ukraine. They married, had a daughter, and moved to an eclectic but modest neighborhood at the bottom of Missionary Ridge, site of the Battle of Missionary Ridge, where the Confederate Army was routed under the Union leadership of Majors Ulysses S. Grant and William T. Sherman.

In 2010, Earl, Natalie, now a medical doctor, Earl, and their daughter moved into a house at the top of the Ridge, where Earl was unofficially the first Black homeowner, and just a short jog away from one of the Civil War monuments honoring the Confederate dead.

During Dmitri's youth in the Ukraine, the Soviet Union liked to show the world that it tolerated religion by publicizing images of old babushkas attending Russian Orthodox services. But, young people who went to church and pledged their allegiance to God over the government were watched. Baptist and Pentecostal religions were not considered denominations but sects, dangerous and cult-like, a threat to the government's hegemony. That was why in the eighties, Dmitri's future mother-in-law, a Pentecostal, hid her Bible, hymns, and other religious materials in a beehive outside her house, removing them only when she held secret church services.

As a young boy in the Ukraine, Dmitri had been interested in attending a military college, but in 1991 when he converted to a Pentecostal religion at seventeen, he became a pacifist and refused to use a weapon. At nineteen, when he reported for his mandatory military service, the recruiters stamped the word "Believer" in angry red letters on the cover of his personnel file. His military service time was doubled from one and a half years to three, and he was sent to work in a brick-making quarry under conditions not dissimilar to a work camp.

By the time Dmitri got out of the military, Ukraine's economy had collapsed under the free fall of a post-Soviet society. Because there were no jobs, Dmitri started his own carpentry business building windows and doors, a skill he'd learned in the military. Every morning and evening while his wife worked as a custodian at a daycare facility, Dmitri took care of the house and their four children. He also made windows and doors, which he would then sell at the local flea market. Then even that work dried up, and his family lived on his wife's meager salary, subsisting on vegetables and fruit from their garden in the summer and potatoes and macaroni in the winter. Worried about his family's future, Dmitri, with the help of his brother who had already emigrated to the States, began the paperwork to leave the country. In 2004, Dmitri, his wife, and their four children arrived in the US as religious refugees.

In 1996, Kual was an advisor to the minister of Warrap State in Sudan. When the minister learned that the main government in the Sudanese capital of Khartoum was planning to execute him, he escaped to Kenya. The Khartoum government found out the minister was not returning, and turned their attention to Kual. They went to his hometown of Tonj, in southern Sudan, but he wasn't there. They sent Kual's friends to find him, but one of those friends who knew Kual was in Khartoum warned him that his life was in danger.

Kual had to flee the country. Kenya's border with Sudan was now closed, so he bribed his way through Darfur to Chad to get to the UN refugee camp in Nigeria. Kual and his wife, who later joined him, were allowed to live in an apartment in Lagos, the capital, instead of at the refugee camp. One day, an entourage of cars brimming with Sudanese officials and some of Kual's coworkers from Chad arrived and began circling the house. Kual's coworkers had reported that Kual, a Christian, had said negative things about Muslims, the predominant religious group in Sudan. A man from the Sudanese Embassy spoke in Arabic, a language Kual was fluent in, but Kual answered in English. The man asked Kual to come with them, but Kual refused and threatened to call the police. When they finally left, Kual called the police, who told the Sudanese Embassy to stop harassing UN refugees. Because of that harassment, Kual and his wife were moved to a refugee camp in a smaller town, and that was where his first two daughters were born.

Born in 1971 in Santa Clara, Cuba, Rolando followed in his father's footsteps, becoming a truck driver. Later he worked as a DJ in the nightclubs, eventually running afoul of the authorities when he was caught playing banned music. Because of their harassment, Rolando got involved with a Cuban human rights organization, the Cuba Independienta y Deolocrática, and began organizing nonviolent protests demanding freedom of expression and human rights. After continuously being arrested, beaten, and tortured for his activism, Rolando was afraid that if he didn't get out of the country, he'd eventually be killed.

In 2004, Rolando applied for political refugee status. But the Cuban government kept issuing him different ID numbers, which complicated his application process, so that he didn't receive refugee status for ten years. Finally on January 31, 2014, he emigrated to Chattanooga.

Salim, a Kurd born in Diyala, Iraq, began his mandatory military service shortly before the Gulf War out. As part of the Iraqi army in 1991, he was captured by American forces and held for two months as a Prisoner of War. During his time as a POW, Salim's English, which he'd learned in school and from TV, improved from communicating with the American soldiers.

Before the first Iraq war in 1991, Salim and his family did well. His wife was a math and kindergarten teacher. He repaired watches and sold food in a small shop. But after 1991, the economy fell apart because of international sanctions, and his family struggled. During the second Iraq war in 2003, Salim became a coordinator and interpreter with the United States Army as an Iraqui soldier, because of his ability to speak English. But then after the US Army left in 2011, Al Qaeda terrorists, knowing he'd worked with the Americans, began phoning his house, threatening his family's life. Once, while Salim was out, men with weapons circled his house. His wife called the Iraqi police, who this time were able to chase them away.

A week after the first incident, Salim received a call from his neighbor, telling him there were men with machine guns on his roof. Again the police arrived and sent the terrorists away, but Salim knew that the next time, or the time after that, he and his family might not be so lucky. Because his life was in danger and because he'd helped the Americans during the war, he applied to emigrate to the States as a refugee. While their status was being approved, the family moved from Diyala to Erbil, the capital of Iraqi Kurdistan. After two years, on December 4, 2013, Salim and his family left Erbil for Chattanooga, Tennessee.

Abril's grandmother was from Oaxaca, Mexico. When her father was killed for his land, the grandmother was forced into an abusive marriage. Worried about their safety, she ran away with her young daughter, Abril's mother, to Veracruz. For years they lived in a one-bedroom dirt-floor house, surviving by selling food on the streets and cleaning houses. Abril's mother married at sixteen, and was soon pregnant. Unable to afford a hospital delivery, she gave birth at home, but the baby girl's umbilical cord was wrapped around her neck, and Abril's older sister died not long after her entrance into the world.

In 1990, Abril was born at home, healthy, and then in 1993, her younger sister arrived. The family realized that soon their subsistence living would not be enough to feed the extra mouths, and so Abril's father, as the patriarch, made the bold, but not unusual, decision to move to the States. Abril surmises he probably got the money to pay the coyote (slang for smuggler) to smuggle them across the border from relatives living in the States. Abril doesn't remember the crossing; she was only three, after all, but she does know she was tasked with holding her baby sister tightly in the dark trunk of a Honda Civic until they made it across into the United States.

II. In Transit

"Everyone staying at the refugee reception center has two stories—the real one and the one for the record."

So begins "The Reality and the Record," a short story by Hassan Blasim, an Iraqi now living in Finland, about the stories refugees tell to survive. The real story and the one for the immigration officer sometimes overlap, diverge, agree. They tell the stories they believe the people making decisions want to hear. As Blasim's narrator says, "The real stories remain locked in the hearts of refugees, for them to mull over in complete secrecy."

When refugees tell me their stories, I'm grateful that they have opened their world to me, and shared some of their joy and pain. I'm always amazed by their resilience and determination. I also know they are telling me the story they tell people they believe have some power over their lives. They tell these stories "for the record" because they depend on our empathy. Their real stories are more complex, personal, unknowable.

But, it shouldn't be the refugee's job to elicit empathy in the listener. Instead, as Paul Bloom says in his essay "The Baby in the Well,"

Our best hope for the future is not to get people to think of all humanity as family—that's impossible. It lies, instead, in an appreciation of the fact that, even if we don't empathize with distant strangers, their lives have the same value as the lives of those we love.

By listening and telling stories, we acknowledge each other's value, as different as our lives are. As one of the characters says in Blasim's story, "The world is just a bloody and hypothetical story, and we are all killers and heroes." With these stories of the world, no matter which parts are true, we can connect and listen to the killers and heroes in ourselves, to acknowledge the value of a stranger's humanity.

III. Arrivals

Once they'd crossed the border into Arizona, Abril's family drifted to New Haven, Connecticut, where some relatives lived. Soon enough, her parents found jobs in restaurants and construction. By the time Abril's brother was born a few years later, her parents managed to get Abril's grandmother across the border to live with them and help raise the children.

But after only a few years in New Haven, Abril's father, fleeing debts and moneylenders, took the family to Raleigh, North Carolina, where Abril's parents picked tobacco for a year. They then relocated to Chattanooga, but soon after that, Abril's father disappeared with their savings and their only car.

Abril's mother worked three jobs, and over time she saved enough money to buy a house. She developed a relationship with a more reliable man, and Abril, her younger sister, and her brother thrived academically and emotionally. But then one day late in 2006, Abril's brother, who was ten, developed a fever that spiked so high he started hallucinating. Soon after he arrived at the hospital he fell into a coma.

Her brother was diagnosed with bacterial meningitis. The doctors told Abril, who translated the horrific news to her mother and grandmother, that there was a strong possibility he wouldn't survive.

Despite the prognosis, Abril's brother did live. But when he came out of his coma, he'd forgotten everything.

"His body forgot how to breathe."

This was the phrase Abril repeated over and over again. It was as if even now, eight years later when she tells me her story, she still can't understand how a body could forget something so vital. Even in the trunk of the Honda Civic, Abril and her infant sister had not stopped breathing.

Her brother learned to breathe again, but he will never be the same. After having fifty or sixty seizures a day, he was diagnosed with Lennox-Gastaut, a severe form of meningitis-induced epilepsy. With a handful of daily medications, the seizures were reduced to a few times per week.

Two years after her brother's illness, Abril turned eighteen, becoming a legal adult but an illegal immigrant. In her high school, Abril had thrived. Not understanding the ramifications of being an undocumented adult, she'd planned on attending college on ROTC and soccer scholarships. As the oldest child, she was the first in her family to finish high school, and she'd hoped to be the first to graduate from college. But as an undocumented adult, she no longer qualified for scholarships and could not attend college in Tennessee.

Instead, for five years Abril worked off-the-books for a restaurant, unsure if her life would ever change. Then in 2012, President Obama wrote a memorandum known as the Deferred Action for Childhood Arrivals (DACA), which enabled Abril to get a social security number and work legally without fear of deportation. More importantly, she was now able to continue her education. Unable to afford the out-of-state tuition that undocumented persons have to pay in Tennessee, Abril registered for a Mechanics Tool Technology program, which would allow her to graduate in one year with a certificate.

The night after my first conversation with Abril, I kept waking up, unable to breathe. I'd take in long shallow breaths, measuring the air and holding it in my lungs until I had to let it go.

I imagine it's how someone feels as they're trapped or dying.

It's not so much a feeling of giving up as a feeling of trying to live.

I interviewed Salim twice. The living room of his rental house was decorated with fabrics and paintings from Iraq and smelled pleasantly of tea and freshly baked flat bread. For the first interview, his wife sat silently with him on the sofa. Their youngest child, in kindergarten, played under the dining room table with a tablet device.

Although he was a well-educated businessman used to managing and consulting, Salim now worked the night shift at Pilgrim's Pride, a chicken processing plant. His wife attended English classes at Chattanooga State Community College, determined to improve her English, her fourth language. His oldest son, who had been attending university in Iraq, was now taking classes at ITT Technical Institute in drafting and design. Salim's middle son was in high school, and his son playing with the tablet would start first grade in the fall.

"This is my country now," Salim said. "No one helped us in our country; no one paid us one cent. Here everything is different. We just want a stable life. I'm comfortable here. We have nice things."

When I visited Salim a second time, he was alone. His eyes were bloodshot, and he moved as if he had just awakened. He shuffled to the living room as if he were sleepwalking. He was polite and nice, but his answers to my questions were short. Finally he admitted he hadn't slept the night before. He'd just learned he and his family had to move out of their rented home by the end of the month because the landlord did not want to continue the month-to-month lease. He was meeting with his Bridge Refugee Services coordinator after he talked with me to find a new place. His optimism from the previous visit had evaporated. His lined face and red-veined eyes showed the deep-set tiredness of someone forever uprooted, unable to make a home.

Salim talked of selling the house he still owned in Erbil (which since our talks had become a city in a tug of war between the Islamic State and Iraq), and using that money to buy a place here, so that his family would no longer wonder when they had to move next. As long as he rented a house, Salim felt he and his family would continue to be uprooted, not knowing when the rent might be raised or a lease not renewed.

"After we move again and I'm settled, I have many more stories to tell you." His family moved, but I didn't meet with him again. I imagine he is telling those many stories to anyone who will listen.

Rolando agreed to meet me two times at Starbucks off Brainerd Road. He liked to meet outside, even in August in Chattanooga, instead of in the air-conditioned confines of the coffee shop. The second time, while we waited for Ediee, his translator, to arrive, I ordered three tall dark roast coffees. Rolando said he usually only liked espresso like he had in Cuba, but that this coffee was good. Just as in our first meeting, he poured several packets of sugar in his coffee, which he then stirred with a spoon.

Once Ediee arrived, Rolando showed me his biography, written like a confession, and a few other files and videos, which he had saved on a CD for me to keep. In one of the videos, a group of people inside the courtyard of a house were holding up signs asking for democracy and civil rights. Rolando is one of those protesters, serious looking, almost rigid. The same video shows an angry group outside the gate, on the street, yelling at Rolando and the other protesters. Rolando pointed out the plainclothes policemen, small microphones attached, reporting on events. He identified some of the pro-Castro protestors, bused in by the government and paid to protest against the organization. The protestors looked stiff, serious, determined, without joy.

When I interviewed him, Rolando had been in the States for six months. He'd just earned his driver's license and now had a car, an old Volvo donated by Bridge Refugee Services. This car to him was freedom. In 2015, I learned that Rolando was a part-time DJ at Chattanooga's recently opened Cuban restaurant.

I asked Rolando if he worried about his mother, who lived alone in Cuba. He didn't worry about her, but he hoped that someday he could bring her over here. He began crying. He couldn't go back to Cuba, and because of that he might never see his mother again. He said that Ediee reminded him of his mother. He wept quietly, dabbing his eyes with the Starbucks napkin. Ediee mentioned what she'd just read in the paper, that a group of Christians (the Yazidis) were trapped on a mountain, surrounded by ISIS, without food, nowhere to go. She began crying, too, saying she prayed they would be okay.

The first time I interviewed Kual at his new house sponsored by Habitat for Humanity, the gate was locked. The eldest of his three daughters, who had been watching through the window, ran out and let me in. The house smelled of what must have been Sudanese cuisine, warm and comforting. After the family introduced themselves, offering fruit and drinks, I sat down in their living room with Kual and his oldest daughter, who was twelve. Both times while we talked, a station broadcasting news from the Sudanese region played on mute.

I asked Kual why he would want to leave Nigeria for the

US. After all, Nigeria was culturally and geographically closer to South Sudan, where he was from. He said that Nigeria was economically and physically insecure, not a place he wanted to raise his three daughters. In his hometown of Tonj and in the parts of Africa removed from contemporary society and wealth gaps, there was little crime or theft. But in Nigeria, now one of the richest countries in Africa, the great income disparity had made crime and corruption the norm. When he again received threats at the refugee camp, his family was moved to the city. He would not allow his daughters to leave their apartment there, because of that danger.

Kual next became manager of a Nigerian's farm. The Nigerian, a wealthy businessman who lived abroad, was worried his wife, who had been running the farm at a loss, was not trustworthy. After the first month, Kual met with the farm owner and showed him the farm had made a profit of six million naira (the Nigerian currency) in one month alone, which suggested that the man's wife and former manager had been diverting the profits. The farm owner sent the wife and their children away and told her she'd never have a say in the farm again. Kual knew that even though she'd gain nothing from it, the wife would target him for revenge.

One morning when Kual was away from his office on the farm, some armed robbers showed up at the main gate on motorcycles. They rushed to the office and broke open the drawers. Kual's guards confronted them and they spoke Arabic, so that the Nigerian robbers couldn't understand what was going on. They called the police, who arrived quickly with the chief. The armed robbers were arrested.

Kual told the UN it was too dangerous to work on the farm, but with assurances from the farm owner and the UN that he would be safe, he returned.

Three months later, a few men arrived at the farm pretending to be customers buying eggs. One of Kual's guards, though, saw them retrieve cutlass knives from behind the fence that bordered the farm. Once again the guard confronted the men and once again the police were called and had to fight the intruders who had been paid by the owner's wife to attack Kual for revenge. At this point the UN refugee program agreed that Kual qualified to emigrate, and his application for political refugee status at the American Embassy was accepted.

They arrived in Chattanooga in February 2010, when one of Chattanooga's rare snows was falling. His family had never seen snow before and they watched it fall in wonder.

In some ways Chattanooga resembles Kual's hometown of Tonj; both are lush, with lots of trees. But in more ways it's different. There's a short dry season in Tonj, but most of the year is wet, allowing residents to grow a lot of food. In Tonj, the inhabitants eat rice, maize, vegetables, and fish, and use water from the Nile River, which runs through the middle of the country.

"There's so many mangoes," he says, talking of the abundance of the fruit in his hometown. "You watch them fall from trees, and you leave the bruised ones on the ground."

You wait for the sweetest, juiciest fruit.

"There will always be a better mango."

Now successfully settled in Chattanooga, Dmitri is a deacon at his Pentecostal church and works as an adjuster and substitute lead man for the packaging machines at Southern Champion in Chattanooga. His three children do well in school and have adapted. They go to the parks, visit downtown, and in his spare time, like a good American homeowner, Dmitri works on his yard and home improvements.

Yet, Dmitri worries about his sister and her family, still in the Ukraine, and would like to get them to Chattanooga. Even now, despite all of his successes, more than ten years after his family left his country, Dmitri still looks at the moon and thinks, "This is the same moon my family in the Ukraine saw a few hours ago." He misses all he's lost.

About five years ago, Earl and his family moved into a beautiful old house at the top of affluent Missionary Ridge with a swimming pool and a view of Chattanooga and the valley below. I've enjoyed those views while playing croquet in the front yard, from the Braggs' covered deck, and while swinging my feet in the cool water of their pool.

No matter which way you drive to get to Earl's house, you can't miss the myriad Civil War memorials and signposts documenting the battles and skirmishes fought on that ridge.

Below Earl's house on the ridge, a half a mile away, is the much poorer and blacker neighborhood of Avondale. One day not too long ago, three young men from that neighborhood were driving around and ended up on the thin sliver of road that snaked up the ridge and spat them out in front of Earl's house. They parked their car, got out, and walked along the road.

On one side of the road was an unfettered, panoramic view of Chattanooga, with its tiny dots of houses and businesses and trees and the river and the mountains, the promise of all that lies beyond.

On the other side of the road Earl was outside his house on the lawn, working in the garden. One of young men finally asked Earl, "You live here?"

"I do," Earl said.

"He lives here," the young man repeated. His words like a prayer.

As the young man wept in Earl's yard, his friends held him to keep him from collapsing to the ground.

Packing It Up and In

We built them on the quad of Virginia Tech's drill field: makeshift tents, a crude harbinger of the world to come. We inhabited them to protest our school's investment in apartheid South Africa. As college students in the eighties, we were looking for something to protest. We felt cheated because we'd been born a decade too late, missing out on the world of our older brothers and sisters, the baby boomers, the ones with real music, real drugs, real protests. They had the Rolling Stones, free love, and LSD. We had Duran Duran, AIDS, and smart drugs. The issues they protested were moral no-brainers: Vietnam, Women's Rights, Black Power. Our issues were flickering shadows cast farther from home: Central America, the Cold War, apartheid. We didn't have Dylan's "The Times They Are a-Changin'" or The Who's "My Generation," but we could dance in clubs to The Specials' "Free Nelson Mandela" and play REM's "Flowers of Guatemala" on the last record player we'd ever own.

Nipping at our heels was Generation X with their business-minded majors hell-bent on making money. They called it the Go-Go Eighties. We called them the Reagan Youth. The Reagan Youth thought our shantytowns and protest songs were pathetic relics of an overrated era. If the Reagan Youth stood for anything, it was the pragmatic belief that money makes the world go round, and that engagement and appeasement were the preferred approaches to reforming distasteful regimes.

We had not quite approached the era of the burned-out ennui of Kurt Cobain, but neither could we abandon our sixties nostalgia. We did not believe it ludicrous to imagine we could eradicate racism and greed in a faraway country by living in tents on a campus lawn. We did not think it hypocritical to address racism in another country, even when we lived in the South.

I believed I was doing my part by falling in love with guys who played music that was supposed to change the world. For a while, as part of my own emancipation, I quit wearing makeup or shaving. As features editor of our college newspaper, I initiated a series on homosexuality on campus—the staff writer who wrote the series would be dead from complications from AIDS by the next decade. I was also a news announcer for our college radio station, WUVT (Hoda Kotb of *Today Show* fame was my boss for a while). Before taping I would rifle through the pages of UPI stories I'd ripped off the feed, cutting and reassembling the ones I'd chosen for my two-minute news moment. One of those stories was about shantytowns and apartheid in South Africa, and only later (Hours? Days? Months? Years?) did I discover I'd pronounced apartheid wrong—*a-part-heed* instead of *ahpart-hide*—because I'd never heard the word spoken before. My moment summed up my generation's middle-class white moment, our in-between generation, protesting terrible things terribly far away that had names we couldn't pronounce because we still knew so little about the world, how terrible it had been, and how terrible it would get.

About the same time (perhaps that very moment) I was mispronouncing apartheid, my future (younger) husband (who had never seen a shantytown nor knew of their symbol of protest across universities in America) had probably just eaten a toasted ham-and-cheese sandwich with the crusts cut off by his family's live-in maid Lena in the wealthy white suburbs of Johannesburg. After that sandwich, he probably went to ride his BMX bike, as he always did after coming home from his private school. He pedaled past the walled mansions with their landscaped gardens and pools the color of the cloudless sky, riding faster than he should have been, but still not fast enough, when his tire hit a hidden rock in the road. He pitched forward into the roadside gravel, landing on another jagged rock that sliced the soft spot above his hipbone. There he would have bled, helpless, except a neighbor, watching him through her property's barbed wire fence, saw him crash and called an ambulance, which swiftly transported him to the whites-only clinic where he was stitched up satisfactorily. A few months later, a manhole cover fell on his pinky, almost severing it. In that case his parents took him to Baragwanath, the black hospital, where after waiting hours for treatment, his finger was reattached. Today all that remains of his hipbone accident is a pale recessed scar, a slash of memory almost forgotten. His pinky, stunted with a permanent crook, is a more visible reminder of that time.

At the end of the semester we packed our tents, left the quad, and went on to other adventures: road trips, summer jobs, permanent relocations. Our protests did not have immediate effect, but in 1990, Virginia Tech's board of trustees voted to divest its 2.4 million dollars in holdings in South African companies, a result of a directive from the state governor. Later, Mandela himself said that the University of California's three-billion-dollar divestment starting in 1986 was significant in toppling South Africa's apartheid government. It is still debated how much impact the student protests had on the universities' decisions across the country to divest, although I think it's safe to say they didn't hurt.

In 2009 my husband and I visited South Africa, a country no longer spurned and boycotted, a Rainbow Nation whose policies of legalized gay marriage and affirmative action are models of freedom and equality. And yet they were still there, the real shantytowns, tucked into townships, away from the sparkling dazzle of the new society. The poor were still black and neglected. What had changed were the nouveau riche, no longer only white. Three years later, as we drove through dying small towns in Mississippi, I thought of those desolate shantytowns in South Africa. Isolated Black communities living in shacks, no water or electricity, abandoned by their country in the name of progress.

What our generation missed about the one right before us was what they protested immediately affected their lives. Like them, we wanted to protest big things, but those big things were far away, their implications on our own lives uncertain and unclear. Why couldn't we have looked around at what was happening in our own world as well, why didn't we have the foresight to see that *1984* had not been bypassed as we believed, only postponed? For back then, even in our little tents, playing our music that was angry at an unjust world, we thought we were safe. We could not have imagined how much students would go in debt to attend our once "cheap" land grant university. We could not have imagined that twenty years later, Seung-Hui Cho would shoot and kill thirty-two students on our campus. We could not have imagined that another protest with tents, this one even more imaginative and daring than ours, would come and go. What I couldn't have imagined was how much beauty and pain around the world I would witness in the next decades. All because I had the luck to be born a person who could live in a tent for a few days, pack it up, and walk away.

People I Know

Students from Middle Eastern Technical University

I.

Shahab from Tehran, a graduate student in linguistics I met in Cyprus, invited me to join his friends to celebrate Nowruz, the Persian New Year, by jumping over a fire and eating lentil soup. When I was back in Chattanooga, he Skyped with my freshman students to answer their questions about Iran.

Salim, an Iraqi Kurd who was a translator for American soldiers. His family was threatened by Al Qaeda, and he and his famly are now political refugees in Chattanooga.

Nahid left Iran long before the Iranian Revolution to study in the States. She became a US citizen, and is now a well-known writer and teacher.

My English literature students in North Cyprus, men and women with abundant hair, living in jeans and faux hiking boots, smoking fearlessly before class. After hearing about another mass shooting in the US, they asked me: Is American as dangerous as it seems?

No, I said. It's more.

Masoud from Abu Dhabi, now a Norwegian, with a doctorate in petroleum engineering. He wants nothing more than to see the Egyptian pyramids.

Fidan, whose name means "small tree," a counseling professor from Ankara who knits and paints. In Cyprus we went to aerobics class twice a week, and on other days we'd take long walks in the olive groves near campus.

Ali, the vice rector at the university in Cyprus, loved Bloomington, Indiana, even more than New York (he lived in both cities). He would play cards with us most weekends.

Çem, the mathematician who'd studied at Oxford, loved to recite poetry in Turkish, Arabic, English, and German. He told me he'd never been to the States but imagined it to be just like *The Simpsons* TV show.

The boys from Indonesia who made a raft out of tires and rope and took us down a river in Sumatra, cooked our food while they squatted in their sarongs in the jungle rain, who asked me if I knew Madonna.

Adnan, a Bosnian refugee, who now is an English professor, writer, and editor in Sweden. We taught together in Hong Kong, and once were on a short story panel at a conference in Little Rock, Arkansas. I remember meeting him on a bridge in Little Rock, the only people outside in the hundred degree heat. I never heard him complain about anything.

My sister-in-law's brother, who let us stay with him during the summer she and my brother married. He still remembers me flossing my teeth on the stair steps to his Ankara apartment.

My sister-in-law's other brother's wife, who, although eight months pregnant at my brother's wedding, performed the traditional Turkish dance with mesmerizing grace.

Her son Mehmet, now a handsome eighteen, about to begin a degree in engineering. His family hopes the world will have calmed down in a few years when he has to do his military service. My sister-in-law Professor Dr. Ozgur Erdur Baker who at the very moment I write this is in Southeastern Turkey working with UNICEF to develop programs for children of Syrian refugees.

My nephew, Deniz, an unexpected and beloved addition to the family. I held him in my arms when he was a few weeks old. The next time I see him, he'll be walking. I wonder what language he'll be speaking? I wonder how he'll greet me, with arms open or with his head turned away?

Sybil Baker, second from left. Willie Johnson, far right

II.

He wasn't my first boyfriend (that distinction went to Warren McDonald just a few months later in kindergarten), but Willie Johnson was the first boy who had a crush on me. This was probably during the waning months of the sixties, only nine years after the Fairfax County school system began to desegregate. Willie was one of two Black kids in our class. We were supposed to be learning to tie shoes, but I'd learned that when I was three, so when Willie offered to tie my shoes for me I let him. Our teacher caught him bowed down, a supplicant tying my shoe. She yelled at us, and threatened to spank me if I let Willie tie my shoes again. I still don't know what it was that upset her: a Black boy stooped over and subservient to the blond white girl or a white girl and Black boy play-acting an interracial romance. Was she trying to protect him or me?

Later in Korea, after my divorce, I ended up becoming involved to varying degrees with three Black men. Whenever I was out with them, the Koreans gave us little attention. I assumed they'd much prefer a Black man be with me, a blond foreigner, than with a Korean woman.

At least two of those American men are still in Asia with no desire to return to the US. Better to be an outsider and a foreigner than to be a Black man in America. The third man was an American who'd emigrated from Trinidad. Once I met him and suggested we take a walk along the wooded paths behind the campus where I worked. He looked at me strangely and followed. In my country, he said, a woman would never invite a man to go into the woods with her.

What I had imagined as safe and neutral—a walk in the woods—he saw as an invitation weighted with danger.

III.

My father was the middle of five children who grew up on a small farm in Possum Valley, Arkansas. Nicknamed Cotton-top for his white blond hair, my father didn't see his first flush toilet until he was twelve. As a boy he'd search the sky for planes, and when one passed him, he'd shield his eyes and follow it, wondering where it would go.

I suppose I got my wanderlust from him. He loved traveling. Every summer we'd hitch our pop-up camper and hit the road for two weeks, burning through my dad's vacation time. My dad saw all fifty state capitol buildings. After they retired, my parents traveled to Korea, China, Turkey, Egypt, Israel, Norway, and dozens of other countries. Even when he was a few months from dying, my dad, chemo-free, was itching to get on the road again. He never made it to the next place on his bucket list: Costa Rica.

Even so, I'm sure my dad would have agreed with me: life takes us places we never dream of going.

But before all that traveling and wide-openness was the antebellum family plantation in Georgia, rumored to have been used in filming *Gone with the Wind*, lost after the Civil War. Once or twice I remember my father reminiscing, saying, if only we still had that family plantation, we'd be living the life of Riley.

I said nothing.

I'm haunted not so much by my cowardice but that I don't remember feeling horrified and outraged by what he said.

I owe so much to so many.

I try to commit to embracing and forgiving this world.

But until I begin reparations, I will not be able to forgive myself.

PART II
Wanderers

The History of the Wanderer

When I was four my family moved from our modest ranch house in Florissant, Missouri, to a larger two-story home on an acre of land in Fairfax, Virginia. This was the seventies, and children were given a lot of freedom as long as we kept to the rules and boundaries established by our parents. In other words, we didn't even have to keep the rules—we just couldn't get caught breaking them.

Our house was at the end of a subdivision behind which were woods and old cabins, meandering trails and creeks, empty fields and farms. Past the forest was the Farmer's Field, where, it was rumored, we would be shot if we stepped on the farmer's property. Across the street, behind our neighbor's house and more woods, was Tribby's Field, another semi-abandoned farm area with a working well, from which if we fell in we'd never emerge.

Despite our natural freedom, everywhere there existed boundaries, places where natural human curiosity was enclosed.

———

In *Paradise Lost*, wandering is associated with the medieval romance, the chivalric knight, the wandering hero. In Milton's epic poem, the meaning of the word locates itself on a continuum from spatial directionlessness to error, or a straying from the law. In Book Two, Satan, despairing his lot, laments, "Those full of pain, this intellectual being / Those thoughts that wander through eternity." Echoing the *Areopagitica*, the concept of wandering becomes intellectualized: "minds that wander beyond all thought and satiety." It has been suggested that this intellectual wandering relates to the ability to read and think without a path or plan, an idea Milton seems to have supported.

In Book Nine, Eve disappears after a disagreement with Adam. She wanders in the garden, and meets the serpent. Adam afterwards admonishes her, "Would thou hadst hearkened to my words and stayed / With me as I besought thee when that strange / Desire of wandering this unhappy morn / (I know not whence) possessed thee." For Eve—and by deliberate, natural extension on Milton's part, for all women—wandering contains shades of both "strange" and "possessed," as if the act were borderline incomprehensible, or madness. Eve, stunned at Adam's accusation, replies, "Imput'st thou to my default, or will / Of wandering, as thou call'st it." One can hear the air quotes when Eve, incredulous, can't believe Adam is blaming her for wandering. The word's darker intonations trap Eve, making her culpable; and as punishment, or perhaps as a kind of contraception, Eve is no longer free to wander. It is for her "own good" that she be constrained by the all-observing God and his first likeness, Adam.

Eve serves as a powerful template for the literary woman wanderer since Milton. Women, it is presumed, ought to remain under a watchful eye; once they wander outside constraint, it becomes a dangerous act, an insurrection against the natural order. A wandering woman not only strays from her prescribed role as mother and spouse, but also puts to question the roles themselves. In Jane Austen's *Pride and Prejudice*, Elizabeth Bennet begins the novel with purposeful walks, such as when she travels to visit her ailing sister, or goes out to read letters and reflect. In her essay, "The Path Out of the Garden," Rebecca Solnit notes that "these solitary walks express the independence that literally takes the heroine out of the social sphere of the houses and their inhabitants, into a larger, lonelier world where she is free to think: walking articulates both physical and mental freedom."

Elizabeth desires the same physical and intellectual freedom that Eve expressed, naturally, in *Paradise Lost*. Elizabeth, significantly, falls in love with Darcy after she is given a tour of his estate, and later tells her sister, "I believe I must date it [falling in love with Darcy] from my first seeing his beautiful grounds at Pemberley." As Solnit notes, "It is not Mr. Darcy but Pemberley, his estate, that begins to change her mind about him, and walking in his park becomes a peculiarly intimate act." Elizabeth falls in love with the grounds of Pemberley, and as an extension Mr. Darcy. At Pemberley she is allowed to wander—within limits, and with constraints—but also without the grim repercussions of her sister Lydia's sexual wandering, which culminates in a ruined reputation and bad marriage.

Toward the end of the novel, when Elizabeth and Mr. Darcy finally go out alone, they're able to admit their mutual love. Upon their return, they are chastised for being late; when Elizabeth is asked where she was, "She only had to say in reply, that they had wandered about till she was beyond her own knowledge." It's a queer turn of phrase and a clear Biblical echo. The novel ends neatly for Elizabeth—she is rewarded with a good and rich husband and an estate she can enjoy the rest of her life—but this crucial moment hints that wandering could have led to confusion and disassociation. Women, as symbolized by Eve, apparently should not follow desire, curiosity, or self-direction too far. Elizabeth's modest redemption of wandering sends a familiar message with it: do not stray from the expectations of society for too long.

In the fifth grade, my girlfriends and I decided, unannounced, to explore an unpaved dirt road we'd heard connected their neighborhood to mine. When we arrived at my house an hour or so later, my parents were waiting, furious and frightened. While we tried not to show how much fun we'd had on our adventure, my parents were on the phone with my girlfriends' parents, letting them know we were safe. "Why did you go off like that without telling anyone?" they asked. That it hadn't occurred to us to tell anyone did not suffice.

Our parents worried about us not just as children, but as girls especially. Empty dirt roads surrounded by forests are places where, under the wrong circumstances, young girls disappear. We were unaware of such dangers, alert only to the excitement an unplanned journey could offer. It was difficult to understand why the adults were so worried. But I knew from then on: excessive wandering would be punished.

When I reached high school, my wanderings gradually ceased. In the natural course of aging and shifting interests, the paths, creeks, and fields were erased from my imagination. Then subdivisions of identical houses appeared in my hometown, taking the place of cabins and wells, a place that encouraged evening jogs under bright streetlights. But the lesson of my innocent, wandering youth remained.

In my twenties, I grew acutely aware of the dangers of walking alone, began to avoid dangerous places, worried about getting lost. Because we'd been warned, there existed a prevailing sense that the responsibility was ours alone: if we wandered too far afield and ran into trouble, it would be our own fault.

Jane Eyre, published in 1847, takes place before 1820, not long after *Pride and Prejudice* appeared in 1813. As in Austen's novel, the term *wander* appears frequently and in varying forms. The story opens with Jane commenting, "There was no possibility of taking a walk that day. We had been wandering, indeed, in the leafless shrubbery an hour in the morning..." However, a few paragraphs later, she confesses, "I never liked long walks," especially in the cold weather. This opening gambit—a movement from inability, and supposed disappointment, to willful distaste—foreshadows her own subversive narrative, from first meeting Mr. Rochester, to her wandering with him in the garden, to self-exile and supposed fulfillment, to the final return home to the maimed Rochester, where she is content to stay. When Jane learns that Rochester's extensive travels included Jamaica—where he married Bertha, the woman in the attic—she remarks, "I knew Mr. Rochester had been a traveler: Mrs. Fairfax had said so; but I thought the continent of Europe had bounded his wanderings." Jane considers Jamaica outside the safe bounds, perhaps beyond that boundary of self-knowledge. Rochester's wanderings also suggest a troubled spirit. After Bertha attacks her brother, Mr. Mason, Rochester ushers Jane out to the garden. "Now here (he pointed to the leafy inclosure we entered) all is real, sweet, and pure," he tells her.

These allusions to Eden are hardly subtle, and it is in this space that Rochester unburdens himself of his secret. "Bitter and base associates have become the sole food of your memory," he says, "you wander here and there, seeking rest in exile: happiness in pleasure—I mean in heartless sensual pleasure—such as dulls intellect and blights feeling." Jane later responds, "A wanderer's repose or a sinner's reformation should never depend on a fellow creature." The next day, Jane returns to her own childhood home to care for the dying Mrs. Reed. "I still felt as a wanderer on the face of the earth," she reflects. Jane and Rochester are bound through their mutual rootlessness, each trapped in a self-imposed exile, searching for home and salvation.

Returning to Thornfield, Jane walks into the "sheltered" and "Eden-like" garden, a place where "one could wander unseen." But Rochester does see her there, and proposes under false pretenses—echoing Eve's seduction. Later, when Jane discovers Rochester's marriage to Bertha, she leaves Thornfield on a "road I had never travelled," lamenting her "drear flight and homeless wandering." A few days later, ill and nearing death from exposure, Jane collapses at the door to what will become her first real home. Once she is nursed to better health, she agrees to tell her house dwellers (who she later discovers are her cousins) "the history of the wanderer," that is, the history of Jane.

Never in *Jane Eyre* does wandering carry connotations of freedom and virtue, as it does in *Pride and Prejudice*. Throughout the novel, Jane yearns to cease her wandering and Rochester believes she will provide respite to his own. Before her cousin John goes to India, he blesses Jane, as one looking over "his wandering sheep—or better of a guardian angel watching the soul for which he is responsible." This is as near as the term comes to virtue. The wandering woman again requires protection, as my friends and I did in my youth, as Eve did in the garden. Facing Rochester once more, now blind and lame from the fire in which Bertha died, Jane fears that he has gone mad. Not so—and the wandering motif is resolved in its final use: "He groped; I arrested his wandering hand, and prisoned it in both mine." The word is trapped in its own sentence by "arrest" and "prison," the very antithesis of the (negative) freedom that wandering presents.

But there is another person arrested and imprisoned—Rochester's wife, Bertha, locked in the attic (according to Jane) for her own good, to contain her madness, to stop her from harming others. Jane's fear regarding Rochester's sanity is physically manifested in Bertha. As a Creole in the British colony of Jamaica, Bertha's identity strays across nations, memory, sanity, and ethnicity in Jean Rhys' contemporary classic, *Wide Sargasso Sea*. Positioning itself as a prequel to *Jane Eyre*, the novel explores the bonded but unbound Antoinette (Bertha), who is declared mad and then forced by her nameless husband to leave the Caribbean for England.

In a notable contrast to the many uses of the word in *Jane Eyre*, *wander* is not used significantly in *Wide Sargasso Sea*, if at all. Yet, perhaps because she and her mother live alone and destitute on the margins of society, Antoinette seems more vividly aware of wandering's many dangers than any of her literary forebears. She polices herself, careful not to leave her home, which had already fallen into decay. "Our garden was as large and beautiful as the garden in the Bible—the tree of life grew there. But it had grown wild." It's a stark counterpoint to Rochester's garden of peace. Antoinette details the smells of death and life in the garden, describing an octopus orchard that bloomed twice a year. "The scent was very sweet and strong. I never went near it." She is a woman who understands the danger of untamed places, spaces outside societal control. Her husband by arranged marriage comes to hate Antoinette, "for she belonged to the magic and the loveliness" of that untended garden.

To forget the beauty of both his wife and the islands, he tries to erase her and all that she represents. "So we rode away and left it—the hidden place. Not for me and not for her. I'd look after that. She's far along the road now." It is not a path that will lead to freedom or enlightenment. It is the road of dissolution, of losing any self that she had. Her husband renames her Bertha, takes her to England, and imprisons her in the attic.

Antoinette/Bertha, at the hands of her husband/Rochester, becomes transformed into a wandering, suffering expatriate, traversing internal space as Rochester does the Atlantic. Rhys has said of her own Jamaican identity, "Am I an expatriate? Expatriate from where?" Since she was forced from her home, Antoinette is more exile than wanderer: unlike Elizabeth, who discovers happiness and achieves a home through well-bounded wandering; unlike Jane, damned to boundless wandering who finally creates her own home. For Antoinette/Bertha, wandering is internal, sexual, and psychological—until her husband fixes her in a state of untetheredness, "arrested" or "imprisoned"; he erases her identity and seals her in the attic, safe from herself, allowing him to wander the world alone.

Rhys thus turns the prototypical wandering wildness inside-out. What's inside becomes the wilderness without. A similarly disturbing transformation occurs in Paul Bowles' novel, *The Sheltering Sky*. The protagonists, Port and Kit, leisurely travel North Africa in an effort to repair their marriage. But Port takes to late-night wanderings; he has sex with a blind prostitute and later contracts a fatal disease. After his death, Kit wanders "deeper into the empty region which was her consciousness, in an obscure and innermost part of her mind." In the course of her aimless travels through the Sahara, a group of Bedouin rape and imprison her. Tennessee Williams, in his 1949 review of the novel, writes:

> From then on the story is focused upon the continuing and continually more astonishing adventures of his wife, Kit, who wanders on like a body in which the rational mechanism is gradually upset and destroyed. The liberation is too intense, too extreme, for a nature conditioned by and for a state of civilized confinement. Her primitive nature, divested one by one of its artificial reserves and diffidences, eventually overwhelms her, and the end of this novel is as wildly beautiful and terrifying as the whole panorama that its protagonists have crossed.

After my husband and I decided not to have children, we quit our stable jobs in Washington, DC, upended our whole lives, and moved to Daegu, South Korea. At the time we thought we'd be away for a year, that we might return to careers and cars and homes in some American city. But instead we decided to stay for another year, and then another, eventually relocating to Seoul. It's a city that lends itself to aimless walks, with sprawling neighborhoods and delightful discoveries around each corner.

Behind our apartment loomed a mountain with innumerable trails, which meandered and reconnected, providing plenty of opportunities to wander alone. Compared to American cities, Seoul offers safety for women, which allowed me more freedom to explore without recrimination or fear—even at night.

Being a white American woman precluded me from some of the more conservative mores of Korean society. Unlike most Korean women, I wasn't bound to the injunction against wandering. I had already strayed from Western expectations of an educated, white thirty-something, so I also lived outside the social world of marriage, house, family, career. Free from both sets of boundaries, I was granted a freedom in South Korea that

I would not have found in the United States. It was a surreal experience. No matter how far I wandered, nowhere did I feel outside my own mind.

This feeling recurred while reading Nell Zink's *The Wallcreeper*. Jonathon Sturgeon, who called Zink's novel the debut of the year, links Zink solidly to her literary precursors: "a thoroughly contemporary personality that somehow hearkens back to the Brontës and Jane Austin [sic] (and Zink confirms that Austen is a reference for *The Wallcreeper*)." The protagonist, Tiffany, is not so much a woman wandering from a home as an expatriate, not just from America and the world it represents, but social convention as well. Her childless marriage is rooted in a loyalty that accommodates sexual infidelity. Like Elizabeth and Jane—and Milton's Eve, to an extent—marriage provides security, but here it allows Tiffany to discover herself; and unlike these earlier models, she strays without fear of repercussion.

When Tiffany loses her husband, she—in stark contrast to Kit—does not descend into madness. Instead she decides to sever her financial and romantic dependence on men. Alone and wanting to stay in Germany, she sells her possessions at the flea market: "When evening came, I walked off and left it. I embarked on my new life." In this new life, she commits to "working selfishly" on educating herself and working to improve the environment. Tiffany offers a new paradigm of the wandering woman: untethered, she is rooted only in her own self, and needs nothing to wander away from. Her independence actually echoes Port's rationale for leaving the US in *The Sheltering Sky*:

How many times his friends, envying him his life, had said to him: "Your life is so simple." "Your life seems always to go in a straight line." Whenever they had said the words he heard in them an implicit reproach: it is not difficult to build a straight road on a treeless plain. He felt that what they really meant to say was: "You have chosen the easiest terrain." But if they elected to place obstacles in their own way—which they clearly did, encumbering themselves with every sort of unnecessary allegiance—that was no reason why they should object to his having simplified his life. So it was with a certain annoyance that he would say: "Everyone makes the life he wants. Right?" as though there were nothing further to be said.

Tiffany's emancipation is more akin to that of male characters, like Port, who are allowed to work selfishly, to wander without the taint of madness; she stands juxtaposed to a long line of female characters who must be selfless, obedient, and thus protected.

In the last few paragraphs of the novel we jump ahead to the present. Tiffany has achieved her goals and still lives happily, and alone, in Germany. Reversing the moral of those earlier novels, her wandering leads her to self-actualization. So sharply unlike Eve, punished for her wandering and for her desires; so unlike Elizabeth in *Pride and Prejudice* and Jane in *Jane Eyre*, who each find their greatest fulfillment in patriarchal constraints; unlike Bertha and Kit, driven mad by wandering too far: at the end of *The Wallcreeper*, Tiffany, by untethering herself from her country, family, and societal expectations, by adopting the traditionally male prerogative to work selfishly for herself, has no need to wander any more. By uprooting and transplanting herself, she has sown her own garden, and marked out home by removing the boundaries. "I had been treating myself as resources to be mined," she realizes. "Now I know I am the soil where I grow." A redemption of Eve on her own terms, she has seduced Satan—and left him. She eats the apple, uproots the tree, and plants it in a garden of her own creation.

————————

My first marriage ended while we were living in Seoul. I decided to remain abroad instead of moving back to the States, and began to work on my writing.

I studied for a month in Prague and then enrolled in a low-residency MFA program. It was a period not unlike Jane's time with her cousins—a difficult journey led to a temporary space in which I could come to terms with my own long-deflected desire. Wandering led neither to madness and enslavement, nor to domesticity, but to personal freedom and fulfillment. It made me feel like I was a child again, sitting on a log by my favorite stream, the green leafy woods a canopy, frogs and tadpoles pushing through clear water.

Wanderings: On Mary McCarthy's "A Guide to Exiles, Expatriates, and Internal Émigrés"

Buddhist temple, South Korea

"In early use an exile was a banished man, a wanderer or roamer: exul."

As I stroll under a canopy of trees on a wide clean path that leads to the rocky shores of the Trail of Tears river crossing in Chattanooga, I listen for the Native American ghosts, exiled. I want to hear the wind wail. I want to hear the leaves crying. I want to be haunted by their eternal longing for home.

The exile waits to return, sometimes forever. McCarthy writes, "This condition of waiting means that the exile's whole being is concentrated on the land he left behind, in memories and hopes." Yet, for the Cherokee bands forced onto the Trail of

Tears from Ross' Landing in Chattanooga in 1838, there is no "there" to return to, for their home has been erased.

"But in recent times it is worth noticing, a new word, 'refugee' describes a person fleeing from persecution because of his category."

These are some of Chattanooga's refugees: an elderly Cuban man I drive to the clinic because his knee hurts and his blood pressure is high; a young woman from Colombia, hair still wet from her shower, I drive to the woman's clinic for her annual exam; a silent woman from Somalia, buried in layers of sweaters and scarves, who looks as if she is sixty, but whose refugee card states her date of birth as five years after mine; an ambitious Iraqi Kurd, whom I drive to take his GED so he can begin college classes; another young man, a Sudanese, who wants to resume his career as a pharmacist.

These refugees have one thing in common: they fled their countries because their lives were in danger.

"The exile is a singular, whereas refugees tend to be thought of in mass."

The artist as exile represents a significant contribution to the Western literary canon, starting with Dante and Ovid and continuing with writers such as Vladimir Nabokov, Herta Müller, Milan Kundera, and James Baldwin. In *Portrait of the Artist as a Young Man*, James Joyce writes that the three conditions for an artist are "silence, exile, and cunning." Joyce himself chose a self-imposed exile from Ireland because he believed his own country would stifle his work.

Czeslaw Milosz, the Nobel Prize–winning poet, considers the personal exile of an artist like himself, who emigrated from Poland to the US in 1960. In his essay, "Notes on Exile," he writes, "Exile accepted as destiny, in the way we accept an incurable illness, should help us see through our self-delusions." In this sense, exile is a type of destiny, because one's personal life is dependent on larger historical forces. Yet, being separated from one's culture presents its own problems. As Milosz says, "Now where he lives he is free to speak but nobody listens, and moreover, he forgot what he had to say."

"An expatriate is almost the reverse. His main aim is never to go back to his native land, or failing that, to stay away as long as possible. His departure is wholly voluntary."

In contrast to exiles who are unwillingly separated from their culture, expatriates often want to flee theirs. Now more than forty years after McCarthy's 1972 essay was published, the term *expatriate* sounds distastefully antiquated and colonialist. Today, as people voluntarily shuttle between and among countries, their values connect them to ways of living rather than the nation-states' terms. As a result, they more often refer to themselves as transnationals, global citizens, and third cultures than expatriates. Even in the sixties, Baldwin, who spent much of his adult life in France, referred to himself not as an expatriate or an exile, but a "transatlantic commuter."

When I moved to South Korea in 1995, I half-consciously had some romantic notions of being an expatriate writer living in self-imposed exile in order to write. My plan to live there for a year turned into twelve, and this changed the course of my life in ways I could not have imagined. Before I moved to South Korea, I was thirty-one, married, and working as a technical writer, living in Arlington, Virginia, with my husband, who had a solid job at Georgetown Law Library. Life was good enough, and our next logical moves were to buy a house and have a child or two and raise a family. The problem was, I'd grown up in Fairfax, Virginia, and hated these very suburbs I was about to commit my future to.

For many people, the suburbs are a place of comfort, stability, and, if they are lucky, community. I found them stifling, alienating, and oppressive. If I'd kept my respectable job and bought a house in the suburbs, I'm sure my feelings would not have diminished. I would have lived one of those lives of Thoreau's "quiet desperation." I felt that quiet desperation already beginning to fall on me, heavy and inevitable. Only some radical changes——our decision to not have children and to live abroad instead——threw me off that looming trajectory.

That first year in Daegu, South Korea, was not one of glorious expatriation or creativity. The Confucian culture was too different from mine, and I missed many material comforts of home, which seemed superficial but were so much a part of my life: live music and art museums and decent wine and cheese. Popcorn. Before I left for South Korea, I was taking advantage of the cultural benefits of living in the DC area. For the two years before we moved, I was at one Smithsonian museum or another almost every weekend, catching a new art opening or historical exhibit. I went to Ethiopian restaurants and French bistros and coffee shops/bookstores and drank microbrews. I went to wine tastings and outdoor concerts and dive bars and music clubs that no longer exist.

That life disappeared when I moved to South Korea in 1995. Instead, I ate Korean food and tried to teach a difficult language to a people who had just emerged from decades of poverty and dictatorship. I drank instant coffee and watched bad Hollywood movies on our VCR and drank watery beer and listened to the same music from a dozen CDs and mixed tapes. I searched for beauty and rarely found it that first year—I saw dirt and concrete and shorn trees and shabbiness. I smelled sewage and kimchi and garlic thick in summer heat. I did not love Korea, and I reluctantly missed home.

That first year was long and exhausting, and I counted the days until we could return to the States. But then, a fellow American suggested I apply for a university job in Korea. I would work fewer hours, get more pay, and have long paid vacations in the summer and winter. I would have time to write and travel, things I wouldn't have if I began working again in the States. I got a job at a university in Ansan, and my husband and I agreed to stick it out for another year.

After that first year, I took a few trips around Korea and in

Asia, and I began to see the beauty I'd looked for that had always been in front of me. Persimmons growing on trees, flames of red leaves lining the streets, the traditional songs like some kind of ancient blues, the serenity of the temples, the smell of meat grilling, of incense. The wonder of walking to work, of getting around a country without a car. And when I went back to the States to visit, I saw some of the ugliness there—the myopic, insular conversations, the solipsism, the commercials on TV aimed at every kind of imagined ailment begging viewers to call their doctor and ask if brand X is right for you. I saw the larger and larger houses and wondered why people would want to live in them. I saw everyone driving into work, chained to desultory desk jobs.

The US was a country with faults, like many others. It was not the best place to live in the world, nor the worst. I loved my visits, but I was happy to get back to my two-room apartment with its heated floors and ovenless kitchen and my earnest, sweet students. Even more, I was eager for my next month-long trip to Mongolia or Burma or Indonesia.

One of Chattanooga's most famous expatriates-in-exile is Bessie Smith, who left Chattanooga to join a showbiz troupe as a singer in 1912, and never looked back. Just as Baldwin had to leave America to thrive, Smith, who lived in poverty in segregated Chattanooga, had to leave the small, restrictive town to become one of the most revered (and wealthiest) blues singers of all time. In some ways Smith helped Baldwin finish *Go Tell It on the Mountain*, which he wrote as an expatriate in exile. In a *Paris Review* interview, Baldwin says of writing the novel:

> After ten years of carrying that book around, I finally finished it in Switzerland in three months. I remember playing Bessie Smith all the time while I was in the mountains, and playing her till I fell asleep.

For writers like Baldwin, a gay African American in post–World War II America, leaving or staying in the US was to him choosing between life and death. After he witnessed his friends either going to jail or committing suicide, Baldwin realized he could not become "a man" if he stayed:

> In my case, I think my exile saved my life, for it inexorably confirmed something which Americans appear to have great difficulty accepting. Which is, simply, this: a man is not a man until he is able and willing to accept his own vision of the world, no matter how radically this vision departs from others.

Leaving the States did not save my life as it did Baldwin's, but in a way it gave me one. I guess I should consider my twelve years in Korea as more of a time of voluntary expatriation rather than chosen exile. I was not escaping anything specific, but I felt more that I was running toward something—a larger way of seeing the world and myself. Not so much a place, but toward a space that allowed me to expand my own vision, as a writer and as a human. What living abroad did for me allowed me to live as an outsider and to see the world, forever, in broader terms. It saved me from despair.

Reverse Migration

Migrants sleeping on a bus   *Photograph by Riley Draper*

After our month-long travels across Southeastern Europe, Rowan and I arrived at my brother and sister-in-law's apartment in Ankara ready for a home-cooked meal. We were (over) fed in typical Turkish fashion: first lentil soup, then homemade dolmas and hummus, feta cheese, various salads with sprigs of fresh parsley drenched in lemon juice, bowls of dark olives, moist flanks of baked salmon, the ubiquitous basket of crusty bread. Then slowly we sipped the thick frothy demitasse of Turkish coffee, eating slices of flourless chocolate cake, distributing the gifts we'd brought, feeding my four-month-old nephew, and placing him in his crib.

Only then did my brother and sister-in-law ask about our travels. In late June, we'd left my family—vacationing in Marmaris on the Aegean coast of Turkey—and flew from Dalaman to Vienna [1]. The flight was uneventful. We didn't even go into the city. Nine years earlier, Rowan and I had taken a train

---

[1] On October 11, Vienna's Social Democrat mayor narrowly won reelection after an unexpected challenge from the anti-immigration right.

to Vienna from Prague after our wedding there. Instead, at the airport, we boarded a bus that took us directly to Bratislava, the capital of Slovakia, a country we knew little about [2].

The Bratislava bus station was not far from the city center. After some aimless wandering, I found a tourist information center where we were given a city map and accommodation recommendations. Rowan and I booked a tiny room in a hotel not far from the city center. It cost sixty euros a night, the most we would pay for a room on our entire trip. With its pedestrian-only compact cobblestone streets where castles and churches dotted the landscape and wine bars and cafés spilled onto the sidewalks, the eighteenth-century town set along the Danube was a miniature version of what Americans must imagine Europe to be.

We had arrived on the day of the annual Coronation Festival, which reenacts the eighteen kings and queens crowned in Bratislava. This year's festival centered around the 1711 coronation of Charles VI of Hungary. More than 150 Slovakian actors in period garb paraded through the streets, banging drums, playing instruments, and cheering. They gathered in the heart of the square. Tourists and locals drank from glasses of white

The Coronation Festival in Bratislava

---

[2] On August 19, Slovakia's Prime Minister said his country would accept only Christian refugees because the country had no mosques for Muslims.

wine from the concurrent wine festival, which began at nine in the morning. For those who couldn't see the stage, a large screen broadcast the long and tedious coronation. The Pope's many rings were kissed. Bible verses were read. Allegiance to God and the nation was sworn.

Rowan and I later wandered those cafés and bars until shortly after midnight, where European couples and British boys on holiday drank cheap bottles of regional wine. The locals were friendly. Perhaps the festival put them in a good mood. The next morning a woman at the front desk of the hotel gave us directions to the train station, and we decided to walk the two kilometers to save the taxi fare.

The train station appeared dilapidated, almost a ruin [3], before we realized we had arrived on the back side of the building. We crossed the rusted tracks, stumbling around broken glass and cracked concrete shot through with dried grass. This side of the train station—ghostly with its abandoned, sloping tram stop shelter—would be filled with the homeless at night. On the other side, a modern transit center hummed with electronic signboards blinking the latest arrivals and departures. Sleek escalators led to two platforms where trains arrived from and left to other European cities. We bought our tickets for Budapest, three hours away. There was no internet service, no English-language newspapers. We waited in a tiny coffee shop, drinking Nescafés and sharing a bag of chips until the train arrived.

Keleti train station [4] in Budapest was both grander and more chaotic than the one in Bratislava. The floors hummed with people trying to get in and out. Overhead a large arched ceiling covered the central part of the capacious, multistoried building. It would be easy to lose one's way in here. Although the city's economy depends on tourism, little English was spoken and

---

[3] The day after the November 13 Paris attacks, the Slovakian PM said, "We are monitoring every Muslim in our territory."
[4] On September 1, Hungarian officials closed the Keleti train station to migrants and refugees en route to Germany.

Érzsebet Square, Budapest

there was only one information booth, at which a middle-aged man behind a plastic window gruffly exchanged our euros at an especially bad exchange rate. Since they didn't offer any real maps, I showed the man the address for our hotel, which I had booked on the internet, and he gestured down the street ahead of us. As we walked down the main street in search of the address, we wondered if it was a mistake.

The apartment, rented for twenty euro a night, was part of a complex with an interior courtyard that required three security codes to access. The room itself was part of a suite. There was a lumpy bed and hole-ridden sheets, a nonfunctioning microwave, and a lukewarm shower. But it also had a fridge and a hotplate and expansive parquet floors. Windows swung open to the noisy streets, giving our lodging the pleasant atmosphere of a struggling boho artist café.

Rowan and I walked for a few kilometers toward the river and discovered the more expensive, cleaned up, touristy part of town, where slim Europeans sipped Starbucks coffee and chilled glasses of fröccs, or wine spritzers. In Érzsebet Square locals gathered and drank cans of beer in the worn patches of grass, sharing crackers and other snacks, legs stretched to catch the last of the setting sun.

I could understand how tourists would fantasize about the city. Baroque, Art Nouveau, and Classicist buildings lined the streets. There were cheap drinks and relaxed, communal public spaces. But random fires burned openly next to trashcans beneath the marble. A woman yelled at Rowan for sitting on an empty bench in front of her shop at the train station. No one spoke of them, but they were there already: quiet, desperate, dark-haired people sleeping on the floors of Keleti station, waiting for trains to Vienna and beyond [5].

Having taken the sleeper to Bucharest, we were unable to locate our hotel. There were no tourist information centers or city maps of any kind at the station. Rowan had written down the name of the subway stop he thought was located near the hotel I had booked online called, wrongly we discovered, City Hotel Bucharest. It had been advertised as one minute from Plaza Romania, and we were optimistic about its location.

However, we got out in some area very far from the city indeed, and after walking around aimlessly, unable to find the street, we finally asked someone and discovered that we were still many kilometers away. We flagged a taxi to the hotel, which, despite its decent reviews, was about an hour from the city center, in a run-down suburban area of town. To get downtown, we walked one kilometer to a shopping center where a tram, for which no one seemed to pay the fare, took its riders to a distant subway station.

Maybe it was because it rained the whole time, or maybe it was the hotel's location, or maybe it was something else entirely, but Bucharest felt strangely deserted. Rowan and I rode a double-decker tourist bus around the city. We never disembarked. One British couple sat in the seats behind us, reading out loud from their guidebook. When we ducked into a restaurant during a sudden rainstorm, we were the only customers, and the waiter

---

[5] In October 16, Hungary shut its border with Croatia, building barbed wire fences across the area.

greeted us warmly and with excellent English. We ate stew under an awning outside the restaurant and watched the water gush down the side streets. When the rain lessened we made the long trek back to our hotel, only to return to the city the following morning, to take the train to Brasov.

With its verdant hills and bucolic farms, Brasov seemed worlds away from the rainy, dingy city we'd just abandoned. We knew nothing about Transylvania, except that Dracula's legendary castle was to be found there, so we were surprised to find that the area is a popular vacation destination for thousands of tourists from across Europe and Russia. Tables lined the center of Brasov's pedestrian street, where visitors and locals ate plates of cake and pastries and smoked. They drank wine and beer no matter the time of day. Carafes of rosé were cheap and refreshing under the hot sun. Boys barely in puberty yet drank beer and smoked cigarettes without shame.

One evening we moved from the outdoor café into a bar that was featuring karaoke, where families and large groups of friends gathered to perform. The highlight of the evening was a Romanian who falsettoed his way through "Staying Alive," followed by another person who sang an off-key version of "New York, New York" with gusto. Later a middle-aged guy with poor posture sang an off-key Tupac's "California Love" with surreal earnestness. His wide gray-and-white-striped polo shirt glowed a queasy green under the disco lights of the club as he sang intently to the lyrics that scrolled on the screened wall.

With day trips to Dracula's castle and the gingerbread-house-style village of Sighisoara, we enjoyed Brasov so much that we kept extending our stay there. Through the graffiti-covered windows of the train I watched the passing bucolic farms where families still traveled by horse and wagon, and I imagined that all the villagers knew each other and didn't need the outside world.

When the apocalypse happens, I thought, these people will be fine. The thought startled me. It seemed to arrive from somewhere else, someone else. What did I know? How many dreamed of leaving, of going to Brasov? How many might be huddled around a street fire in Budapest? My fantasies revealed a chasm between worlds, one of my own ignorance.

An abandoned building in Bucharest

After five days in Brasov, it was time to take a train back to Bucharest and fly to Thessaloniki. Only a few weeks remained before we were due back in Turkey.

Thessaloniki came alive in the evening, with Greeks filling the coffee shops and restaurants next to graffitied ruins until the early morning. The country was on the brink of defaulting on its loan to the European Union, and possibly being kicked out of the EU. The banks were closed, but ATMs would spew cash for anyone with a foreign bank account; Greeks waited in long lines to withdraw their fifty-euro daily limit.

The city looked depressed, but not defeated; I had seen many towns in the States similarly shuttered, towns that had little chance of the comeback that Thessaloniki held. Though not the town itself as much as the people. A Greek man bought a boy who suffered from a club foot a little simit (sesame seed roll), and together the two strangers observed a passing woman in a dress with bold blocks of color. She had tanned skin, large gold hoop earrings, and wedge shoes, and I noticed as well how she stood out, an avatar strolling the promenade next to the sea as the town clock struck.

Rowan and I rode another bus to Alexandropoulos, where we took a ferry to the rocky island of Samothrace. In the village of Therma, where we stayed, we ate fresh fish and black goat, the specialties of the island. The crisis had driven away most of the tourists, yet because Greece's currency was the euro, the locals could not lower prices as dramatically as in the non-euro countries we'd traveled in. On July 16 [6], we crossed the border back into Turkey on a private bus, spending two nights in Istanbul before flying to Cappadocia, where fairy chimneys and ancient dwellings were carved out of the sandstone rocks of the landscape itself. In the mornings, before it was too hot, balloons drifted across the old cave monasteries whose ceilings still bore chipped, faded paintings of Jesus.

The hotel's breakfast was a pleasant if predictable spread of assorted meats and cheese and yogurt. One older couple—he hanger-thin, she in her headscarf and as broad as a babushka—shared large plates of sliced bread, ham, cheese, and olives. They seemed the type of old couple who had been married for years, who had shared the whole of their one life together, enjoying a vacation now that the kids had grown. But one morning Rowan had breakfast alone. He told me that the couple had been down there eating massive amounts of food. Plates piled high with meats and cheeses. Gorging themselves. An hour later, when I went down to eat, they were there, still eating.

With their conservative, faded village attire, they suddenly didn't look like tourists at all.

My brother asked if I had gained any particular insights. I said no. Had I lied to my brother? Or to myself? We said goodnight.

---

[6] On July 16, a few miles from my home in Chattanooga, a young man opened fire on two military facilities, killing five.

Musicians outside Ankara Castle

Rowan and I slept in the spare room. Lying in bed, I thought about the trip. There had been no air conditioning in the rooms where we stayed, and for inscrutable reasons, nobody believed in fans, so I got used to sleeping with the windows flung open for a hopeful breeze. At night my hair stuck to my neck, and we could hear sirens and arguments and neighbors gossiping outside, all their windows open as well, and then in Turkey we heard too the pre-dawn call to prayer.

In the mornings the sun would sear the room, wherever we were. It seemed to be stalking us. Rowan and I each wore the same few shirts and shorts with sandals or sneakers, possessions pared down to what could fit into a backpack or gym bag. Rowan would occasionally fill shower stalls or bathtubs with water to swish and wring the filthy clothes until the water clouded over. Then we laid the clothes in the sun to crisp dry in an hour. And as I lay there, not sleeping, wondering if I had any insights, my shoulders ached from days of carrying a backpack in the relentless heat.

Back in Ankara, Rowan and I took the subway to Ulus [7], the old city of Ankara, hiking up the hill to the thousand-year-old Ankara Castle, which overlooked the city. Somehow we lost the way, ending up on the streets of non-tourist Turkey. Over so much travel, the intentionality and fiction of tourist Europe had erased these places from our imaginations. Women in head-scarves pinned clothes to a line, and children stared from their compact houses. Tiny minarets and mosques called to prayer, competing in an ethereal echo. Trying to find our way, we asked a man blocking what remained of the dusty road. He raised his hands. No, he said, over and over, and directed us to turn around. Finally, we made it to the top, where the Turkish flag whipped in the wind, and men played traditional songs against the castle walls for change.

Then, before returning to Istanbul [8] to fly out to Atlanta, Rowan and I, accompanied by my brother and his wife, went on one last trip to Beypazari [9], a small town outside Ankara known for its local jewelry, Ottoman-era architecture, and an annual carrot festival. There had been a fight just before we arrived. The streets were blocked, filled with smoke. People were shouting. The police had arrived already. We didn't know what had happened. As the smoke cleared, we watched along with the rest of the bystanders as the police shoved a man into their car and sped down the street. Quickly the people resumed their daily routines.

I bought an earring and necklace set of silver filigree for my mother-in-law, and we ate a pleasant meal outside in a restaurant that overlooked the town: soup and salads, lamb served in a clay pot, baklava and Turkish coffee. In the parking lot, a small dark-haired boy in ragged clothing came up to us, his hand thrust out,

---

[7] On October 10, at the nearby bus station, an explosion killed 100 protesters at a peace rally.

[8] On December 1, two pipe bombs injured five at an Istanbul metro station.

[9] On September 8, pro-Kurdish protesters clashed with police in Beypazari, resulting in seven wounded.

speaking a language that wasn't Turkish. Another boy, perhaps his brother, who was a few years older, watched quietly before joining in, both his hands outstretched, and then a girl, the oldest, emerged. Around five, seven, and nine, maybe siblings, hard to know to know for sure; they could have been younger.

I had encountered destitute people of all stripes along our trip, the unacknowledged texture of modern cityscapes. On the streets and at the train station in Hungary and in Romania, signs in English implored us not to give money to beggars, that there were programs for them, that giving money did not solve the problem, that it encouraged dependency or worse. Women on sidewalks holding babies, stray children, the man in a wheelchair in Thessaloniki; and back in the States, the man who sleeps under the bridge across from our house, in one of the better neighborhoods.

We didn't know about the extent of the Syrian refugee crisis then. But these children almost certainly were three, just three, of the millions that have been dispersed, drowned, deterred, resettled, or left in camps. Over the following six months, hundreds of thousands would make their way by boat and train and road from the Turkish coast to the shores of Greece to Romania to Budapest to Bratislava to Vienna. They would follow our path, in reverse, until the fences and closed borders forced them back. Had we not seen them at all? Had we chosen not to see? Behind the too-clean squares, the festivals, the cafés and restaurants, the police, along the train lines and the bus routes, had we been among them all along?

We didn't know if those children had a mother or a father, or were orphans, something in between, or worse. We didn't know what they had seen. My sister-in-law, Ozgur [10], reached for her wallet, and offered them a ten lira note; I only had a few coins left. It was nothing. Even now I'm embarrassed by how little

---

[10] On December 8, Ozgur, my-sister-in law, went to Southeastern Turkey to help UNICEF develop programs for child refugees. Close to two million Syrian refugees were still in Turkey.

we gave. For a moment, though, the youngest boy was bursting with joy, though the brother looked through us unmoved. The older boy, just old enough to understand how the future draws its outlines from the present, and what that means for them. His eyes, implacable and dark: he is trapped here, and for no reason other than luck and the lack of it, I am not.

No Exit

I. The Tourist Information Kiosk
Will Be Closed Due to "Stuff" Cut

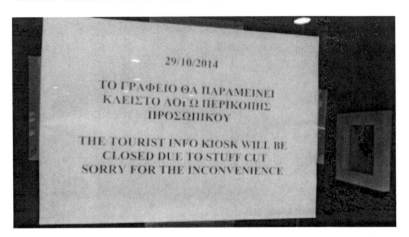

Three days after 61 percent of the Greeks voted OXI (no) to accept a proposed bailout agreement, Rowan and I bought plane tickets from Bucharest to Thessaloniki. We were several weeks into our travels around Southeastern Europe, and our plan was to travel overland from Greece to Ankara, Turkey, where my brother and sister-in-law lived with their four-month-old son. Without a bailout, Greece would default on its loan, and possibly exit the EU. We'd seen the TV footage of the Greeks standing in lines at closed banks, angry groups rioting in Athens, stores empty of food. While we were touring Dracula's castle in Romania, some British tourists suggested that we bring lots of euros in cash, because we wouldn't be able to get any money while in Greece. News announcers warned that unless a deal was made soon, chaos was imminent.

We wanted to go anyway. We didn't believe that Greece was that dangerous. We were curious. We needed to get back to Turkey. Traveling overland through Greece seemed to be the cheapest and most interesting option.

But when we arrived at Thessaloniki's airport, I wondered if we'd been a bit too cavalier in our decision. We were greeted not by humans but by a computer printout announcing the tourist kiosk's year-long closure, its sad spelling error not even corrected. A shuttered tourist kiosk at the airport of Greece's second-largest city seemed foreboding. A city that could not afford the one thing that might bring in money was a city beyond help.

Besides, we needed help, too, in the form of advice, maps, and directions. To keep our backpacks light, we hadn't brought a computer or a guidebook along, so we were dependent on internet cafés to check email, research travel options, and book hotel rooms, which, thanks to the smartphone apps we didn't have, had become unfashionable since our last visit to the region in 2006. In Budapest, for example, the only internet café was on the second floor of a dusty shop run by an elderly man, with pre-millennium computers hooked to dial-up modems that could barely load the search engines, a place that reminded me of the shop and upstairs bedroom where Winston was caught by Big Brother in *1984*.

From the airport, we found a city bus that would take us to where we'd booked our hotel, allegedly in the heart of Thessaloniki, that at forty euros a night, breakfast included, was within our budget. Because we didn't have a map and because there was no tourism office at the airport to provide one, we had to guesstimate where to get off. We knew the White Tower was one of the major landmarks in the city, so we figured our hotel must be near there. I'd foolishly assumed that, despite the EU crisis, public transportation would be running and would get us across the border into Turkey, but now, as the bus tumbled past trash-strewn streets and boarded-up buildings, in a country possibly on the brink of economic collapse, Ankara and my four-month-old nephew who lived there felt unreachable.

The bus dropped us off at the White Tower. Mapless, we tried to get our bearings. It was midday and the city was hot, dusty, and drained of color, but we had no choice other than to start hoofing the pavement toward what we believed was the address of our hotel. As we passed the dozens of closed storefronts, the cafés packed with denizens nursing one-euro iced coffees, we noticed the graffiti—on walls, windows, statues. The graffiti of despair, of the silenced. OXI. Although most of the graffiti was in Greek, a few slogans were in English, aimed, we guessed, at the ever-dwindling numbers of tourists.

The graffiti reminded me of the writing on the walls in the boarded-up house we'd thought about buying in Chattanooga the year before. How, when I'd entered the last room of the ramshackle abandoned house, the wall was magic markered with someone questioning why they should go on living. And this, all over the city, was what I was seeing now.

II. My Friends Are Making Art and
I Don't Want to Leave the House

The next few days we ventured out in the mornings after a breakfast of bread, sliced white cheeses, salami, and Nescafé. The tomatoes, cucumbers, olives, and fried eggs we'd get with our Turkish breakfasts were missing, now an extravagance. Then we'd walk the empty streets, past open-air ruins that, if they hadn't been in competition with the rest of Greece, would have been a major tourist attraction. The streets were marked with half-excavated ruins of the ancient city, whole sections of villages buried and awaiting discovery. There was no money, though, to excavate that past while the present was also crumbling.

The Greeks didn't emerge from their darkened apartments until afternoon. They'd fill the cafés, where they drank Café Freddos (iced coffees) and smoked, discussing, one guessed, the future of the country they lived in. The newsstands sold about twelve different newspapers, a different flavor for each political leaning, but none were in English, so we remained relatively clueless about the intricacies of the bailout debate. At night, the same talking heads, all men, dominated the TV stations. As with the graffiti, we could only guess what was being discussed. In the later afternoon, the city would quiet again. I assumed people retreated from the heat, perhaps to jobs, perhaps to their apartments.

There was, to our relief, a very nice tourist kiosk at the city center, but it was closed on the weekends (we arrived on a Saturday) and we had to wait until Monday to visit it. A nice young man with excellent British English gave us a sheaf of brochures and maps we no longer needed. We boarded a city tourist bus, for only two euro, which drove us from the coast to the top of the hill in Thessaloniki and back down in forty-five minutes. From the speakers, a professional pre-recorded woman with a British accent described the famous ruin or museum or neighborhood as we passed. But the British-accent lady was mostly sidelined by an earnest myopic man who'd taken our tickets. He read straight from a guidebook, his taped glasses pressing desperately close to the pages. His Greek accent was thick and his message even more canned than the recording. At the end of the tour we filled out poignant tourist evaluation forms, since there were only four of us on the tour, and the worst of the Greek crisis was yet to come. We gave our guide 5 out of 5 across all categories, hoping good reviews might delay the inevitable elimination of his redundant position.

In addition to Thessaloniki having been occupied by the

Ottomans, Ataturk, the father of modern Turkey, was born in Thessaloniki. His house was still standing and available for touring, although the Greeks didn't mention this in their tourist materials. It seemed that many of the Greeks still had not forgiven the Turks, and vice versa, to the economic detriment of both countries. That meant that Turks came to Thessaloniki to see Ataturk's childhood home, but that the Greeks would rather the home would disappear. There was no way to see the house unless you had a car, so Rowan and I gave it a miss.

Even at seven or eight in the evening, the sun burned as if it were midday, keeping the Greeks inside their homes for hours. Rowan and I were the only ones who seemed to have an appetite before dark. Strangely, the wine and beer at all the cafés were four or five euros for a glass, an exorbitant price compared to the other countries we'd been in. In Romania, where we'd just come from, we'd been particularly spoiled by three-euro carafes of quaffable wine and afternoon drinking. Finally, along Thessaloniki's waterfront we found a restaurant that served white wine by the carafe and provided miniature buckets of ice, which Rowan was always on the lookout for. We ate satisfying meals of fish and fried calamari and Greek salad, and only at nine did the first Greeks appear on the promenade as the sun was finally beginning to set, allowing the evening to slightly cool. We'd wind our way back to our hotel just as the others were emerging for dinner, morning and nocturnal animals crossing paths. Despite or because of the apocalyptic times, the Greeks partied well into the early morning, which was one of the reasons, we guessed, it was hard to find a shop open before noon.

Rowan, who wouldn't drink anything without ice, would wander the neighborhood groceries and convenience stores, trying to find some. Finally, at one store that had again refused him, he laid a euro coin on the counter. The man disappeared and returned with a bag of ice he'd mysteriously found. We quickly learned the power of the euro coin.

III. Fuck Gold Fuck Money Fuck Capitalism

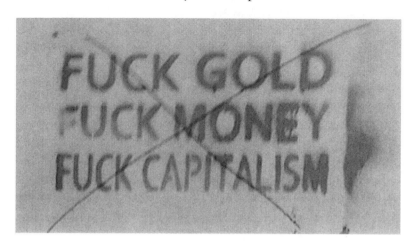

The day after Greeks and creditors agreed to a bailout of eighty-six billion euros imposed under extreme austerity measures, we took a bus to Alexandropoulos, a coastal city not far from Turkey's border. We got off in the city, again unsure of where to go, so we followed the backpackers who had been on the bus to a ticket booth near the pier, and bought tickets for a boat to the island of Samothrace, where we'd booked a room in a small hotel promising breakfast and a view of the sea from our balcony.

The ferry was packed with hundreds of locals and twenty-something tourists from non-English-speaking countries: Italy, Greece, Bulgaria. I was reminded of the scene from almost twenty years ago on Bangkok's Khao San Road. Then and now, the neohippies wore baggy cotton pants and bandanas and brought sleeping dogs. They smoked cigarettes and were lean and hungry looking. It was impossible to envision what they'd look like ten, twenty years from now—rich and fat perhaps, with families and vacation homes if they were lucky, or maybe they would be eternal drifters, forever scraping by. When we arrived on the island, everyone except us scattered to taxis and cars waiting for them. We followed a group of backpackers to a bus, but it looked chartered and we didn't know where it was going, so we did not board it. Once the bus left, there was nothing to take us anywhere.

Our hotel was twenty kilometers away in the tiny town of Therma, but we had no idea how to get to it. We approached a man renting scooters and motorcycles, and, perhaps cunningly, he gave us a ride to Therma, saying to call him if we wanted to rent a scooter.

The town had a few stores and restaurants, and a few make-shift stalls sold versions of what I'd seen in nineties Asia: burlap backpacks, cotton shirts and dresses, wallets and bags with marijuana leaves sewn on them. Young faux hippies from the ferry sat in the outdoor café, playing guitars and smoking ciga-rettes. At night while Rowan and I slept, I imagined all kinds of Greek-style debauchery going on, with guitars and drugs and DJs, because for most of the day, like the mainland, our village was fast asleep. The next morning we learned there was no break-fast with our room after all—the Greek crisis had resulted in a 70 percent drop in tourism so there weren't enough tourists to make breakfast for. We had to wait until noon for our typically Greek owner to awake, bleary-eyed and hair mussed, to make us coffee, Nescafé for Rowan, Greek-style for me.

In the afternoon we followed a pencil-thin trail to the much ballyhooed waterfall, and there we found a straight-man's utopia: people standing under thin waterfalls and swimming in tiny pools of water, women in sarongs washing dishes in a stream, dogs languorously lounging, lithe naked people sunning on rocks, peeling bananas, nymph-like. In reality, the tiny waterfall was only a trickle; the thermal pools were fetid and scummy. And besides, why in the underground fuck-the-EU economy were the women still doing all the cooking and cleaning while the guys were playing guitars?

Bored and slightly disappointed, we caved in and rented a scooter. We spent a day exploring the craggy cliffs and open, empty roads. We toured the Garden of the Gods, still under extensive excavation, which disappointed Rowan, who after viewing ruins in Ephesus, Cyprus, and Thessaloniki on this trip had become a bit of a ruin snob. In the early evenings, our owner, now properly awake, was happy to tell us his take on the Greek crisis. The Greeks, he told us, should have exited the EU two years earlier when the crisis first hit, but now it was too late. To leave now would be a disaster. For example, although Greece made milk, the milk containers were from Israel. If the Greeks left the EU, then they wouldn't have a currency to pay for the milk packaging. The irony was not lost on them, as the owner reminded us. Even though the Greeks had founded democracy in Europe, Europe now wanted to kick them out. Germany had screwed them over. But our owner was also quick to remind us of Greece's resiliency. Greece was after all the land of Homer and Plato and Socrates and was known as the cradle of Western civilization. Our owner had traveled around Europe, and still could say with certainty that Greece, with all its problems, was the only place he wanted to live. They would, he assured us, endure.

On the day we were to leave the island, the owner gave us a ride to the pier, where we caught a ferry back to the mainland.

"What do you want us to tell people about Greece?" I asked him.

"Tell them to come," he said. "We will survive. This is the best country in the world."

IV. Against Prisons and a Society That Builds Them

There is a gift to not remembering much of the past; just ask Odysseus. After he and his son Telemachus slaughtered all the suitors for being bad guests in his house, the suitors' fathers were ready to return the favor. Blood vengeance was imminent. But Athena, who loved Odysseus, intervened, casting a spell so no one remembered the killings, obviating the need for revenge.

There is much I don't remember about past trips and relationships, and because of that, old wounds don't haunt me the way they do some people. I'm quicker to let go of things, to not hold grudges. One could say my nonattachment, the lack of stickiness of my memories, has allowed me some superficial peace. For all of my traveling, I remember little of the specifics of many of my trips. I don't remember, for example, that in 1997, after my brother and sister-in-law's wedding, I spent a day in Thessaloniki and saw Ataturk's home. I remember only taking a train from Istanbul to Thessaloniki and then to Athens. But something happened between 1997 and 2015, and the border between Turkey and Greece, frenemies during the best of times, was more difficult to cross. There was no train and the public bus stopped at the border, where we would have to cross by foot and just hope to catch a bus on the other side. At a tourist agency we learned of a private bus that took people to Istanbul for fifty euros each, which we were happy to pay.

V. No Borders No Nations

Our last morning in Greece, after our hundredth breakfast of bread, cheese, and Nescafé, we waited at the designated pickup stop in Alexandropoulos for the bus to emerge from the busy traffic. The Greek Parliament, after sackings and reshufflings, voted to accept the first round of bailout measures. The second set of bailout measures would be approved in a few days.

After an hour in the brutal sun, the bus still had not arrived. Rowan went to the agency where we bought the tickets.

It is coming. It is coming, the agent said with a wave of her hand, never a good sign. We learned that our bus had been involved in a "minor" accident, and although they were going to have to cancel the bus (No! We'd already booked a nonrefundable night for fifty-four euro at the five-star Retaj Royale in Istanbul!), they'd managed to work out the issue. The bus was coming. There was nothing to do but wait.

By then it was noon and we were hungry. The only place open at that godawful early time was an empty gyro shop, and there I ate my one hundreth gyro, stuffed with lamb and fries. I would gain six pounds on the so-called Mediterranean diet in these few weeks of traveling. Another hour crept by. People in banged-up cars in thick traffic chugged past us. In despair that the bus would never arrive, we discussed alternatives. Taxis were few and far between, but we wondered if we could pay one to take us to the border. We imaged the border to be like that between North Cyprus and Cyprus, which contrary to the rumors and warnings of our Turkish friends, was stunningly easy to cross by car and foot.

Rowan asked a woman who flagged down a taxi, and the driver told us the rate was fifty euro to get to the border, but then we were on our own. But an empty taxi never arrived for us to flag down, and we discussed returning to the bus station and taking a bus to the border, of getting a refund for our ticket. In that small way the gods were with us, because we later discovered there was no real transportation on the other side of the border. The travel agency stalled in refunding our tickets, saying the bus was stuck in traffic, but that it was coming. We'd also failed to note that Ramadan had ended that day, and people were going to Istanbul to celebrate, making traffic even worse.

Three hours late, our bus arrived, already full of passengers. We were greeted by a Turkish driver and ticket taker, who gave us our free coffee and cake as the journey to Istanbul started. I felt like I was already there.

VI. Our Freedom is Your Nightmare

The border crossings took much longer than we'd anticipated. On the Greek side we disembarked at a small duty-free shop where it seemed most people were stocking up on booze. Alcohol used to be cheap in Turkey, but the ruling government's conservative move to discourage drinking meant that alcohol was taxed so much that even Raki, the national drink, was no longer affordable. After about thirty minutes we got back on the bus, our passports returned with the Greek exit stamp. The bus rolled a few hundred meters to the Turkish side, where we again disembarked and surrendered our passports. When it was time for us to re-board, the Turkish immigration officer informed me that I needed a new visa. I gently pointed out that my 180-day visa had not expired, and that I was scheduled to fly out of Turkey before it did. He scoured the pages, counted the days on his fingers, then finally waved me through. I was the last person back on the bus, and its doors closed as soon as I got on.

We were back on the road, still three hours from Istanbul, but, God willing, we would make it to the Retaj and its steam room and sauna before that night's last call to prayer.

What We Learn From Their Bones

Who will I be like when the air runs out? Perhaps I'll be a garden fugitive from Pompeii, flash baked before the fumes can kill me.

Or maybe I'll be like my father, body choked with cancer, and suffocate in my sleep. Or if I'm lucky, I'll die like my Italian friend Silvia, whose last words to those who tried to save her were: *Testa di cazzo.* You assholes. Perhaps that was what they were thinking, those who did not heed the warnings, the ones who hid in the basement storeroom full of pomegranates, the merchant unwilling to part from his wares, the pregnant woman whose bones were green from the gold she wore, sisters twinned by syphilitic disease. They must have blamed the Gods for raining ash on their city, the one they refused to abandon.

Or maybe I will be my horrible self, running at the first sign of danger, leaving you, hand extended, to curse, not the ancient Gods, but instead, me and my kin.

Works Consulted

Books

Austen, Jane. *Pride and Prejudice.*

Baldwin, James. *The Fire Next Time.*

Blasim, Hassan, and Jonathan Wright. *The Corpse Exhibition and Other Stories of Iraq.*

Bowles, Paul. *The Sheltering Sky.*

Brontë, Charlotte. *Jane Eyre.*

Coates, Ta-Nehisi. *Between the World and Me.*

Milton, John. *Paradise Lost.*

Rhys, Jean. *Wide Sargasso Sea.*

Robinson, Marc. *Altogether Elsewhere: Writers on Exile.*

Wheeler, Josephine Dorsey. *The Eureka Straightening Comb.*

White, Helen Baker. *The History of the Baker Family.*

Zink, Nell. *The Wallcreeper.*

Essays, Articles, and Websites

Bloom, Paul. "The Baby in the Well." *New Yorker*, May 20, 2013. Web.

"Chattanooga Next: Moving Beyond Good Intentions." Chattanooga Organized for Action, July 19, 2016, Web.

Chilton, Ken. "The Unfinished Agenda: Segregation & Exclusion in Chattanooga, TN, and the Road Towards Inclusion." *Chattanooga NAACP*, August 28, 2015. Web.

Coates, Ta-Nehisi. "The Case for Reparations." *The Atlantic*, May 21, 2014. Web.

Cohen, Rick. "Chattanooga: A Model of Urban Revitalization, or Inequality and Gentrification?" *Nonprofit Quarterly*, October 9, 2015. Web.

Greenhouse, Steven. "Low-Wage Workers Are Finding Poverty Harder to Escape." *The New York Times*, March 16, 2014. Web.

Honerkamp, Nick. "Honerkamp: Whatever Happened to Citico Mound?" *Chattanooga Times Free Press*, March 1, 2015. Web.

Hubbard, Rita Lorraine. "John G. Higgins, Entrepreneur Extraordinaire." The Black History Channel. Web.

Knapp, Courtney Elizabeth. *Planners As Supporters and Enablers of Diasporic Placemaking: Lessons from Chattanooga, Tennessee.* Diss. Cornell U, 2014.

"Mapping Inequality: Redlining in New Deal America." Web.

McClane, Joan Garrett, and Joy Lukachick Smith. "The Poverty Puzzle." *Chattanooga Times Free Press*, March 2016.

McClane, Joan. "Chattanooga Activists Call for More Diversity in Local Philanthropy." *Chattanooga Times Free Press*, August 7, 2016. Web.

Smith, Ellis. "Seven-Story Housing Development Marks Start of Race to Redefine Historic M.L. King Boulevard." *Chattanooga Times Free Press*, September 19, 2014. Web.

Thomas, G. Scott. "Ratios of Low-Income Households to High-Income Households in 102 Major Markets." *The Business Journals*, January 31, 2014. Web.

Acknowledgments

Many thanks to the editors of the publications where earlier versions of these essays were previously published: "The History of the Wanderer" and "Reverse Migration" in *The Critical Flame*; "Packing It Up and In" in *Defunct*; "What We Learn From Their Bones" in *The Compressed Journal of the Arts*; "The Adventures of a Fake Immigrant" in *Two Thirds North*; "No Exit" in *Origins*; "Excavations" in *Blue Mountain Review*; "Wanderings: On Mary McCarthy's 'Guide to Expatriates, Exiles, and Emigres'" in *Electric Literature*; "Schemers" in *4ink7*; "Landings" in *The Tishman Review*; and "Brief Histories" in *SPOUT*.

The first photo in "Reverse Migrations" is ©Riley Draper. The other photos in "Reverse Migrations" and "No Exit" are ©Rowan Johnson. The photo in "People I Know" is ©Altan Öztürk. All other photos were taken by or provided by the author.

This collection of essays started with a 2014 MakeWork Grant to write about Chattanooga's unheard voices. To say that this collection would not exist without this grant is an understatement. I am also grateful to the Tennessee Arts Commission for awarding me a 2017 Individual Artists Fellowship based on several essays in this collection.

I am grateful to Caleb Ludwick, Chad Prevost, Kerry Howley, Amy Wright, Dana Shavin, Ira Sukrungruang, Jessica Miller, and Beth Partin for their input on various drafts of the essays.

Thanks to UT Chattanooga, Rivendell Writers Residency, Firefly Farms, and Gerald Weaver and Lily Chu for providing space and time for me to work on the manuscript.

Thanks to friends and family from around the world for providing perspective and hospitality: my Turkish family, Derek, Ozgur, and Deniz; Fidan Korkut and Dean Owen for taking me under their wing in North Cyprus; my South African family, Lee, Lorraine, Kyle and Bianca Johnson, and Sam Dwyer; and the Bakers in Williamsburg, Virginia, Arlene, Burt, Stefanie, Ian, and Grant. I'm grateful to my good friends George and Anita and Earl and Natalie and for them allowing me to write about them and our friendship.

Thanks to Richard and Brooke Booker for helping make our house a home. Thanks to Bob Boyer for his patience and support in helping me take some of these photos. Thanks to Salim Latif, "Dmitri," Kual Ayai, Rolando Garcia Casadevall, and Abril for giving up their time to tell their stories to a complete stranger. Thanks to those in Chattanooga for sharing their time and knowledge: Marina Peshterianu at Bridge Refugee Services, Jefferson Hodge at Chattanooga Organized for Action, and Terry Davis at UnaVerSoul Vibes.

Finally, as always, thanks to Rowan Johnson, partner in crime, for your unconditional love, feedback, and support. You make everything possible.

About the Author

Sybil Baker is the author of *The Life Plan, Talismans,* and *Into This World.* She is a UC Foundation Associate Professor at the University of Tennessee at Chattanooga, and teaches at the Yale Writer's Conference. She has received two Make Work Artist Grants and an Individual Artist Fellowship from the Tennessee Arts Commission. She is Fiction Editor at *Drunken Boat.*

OTHER C&R PRESS TITLES

FICTION

Spectrum
by Martin Ott

That Man in Our Lives
by Xu Xi

A History of the Cat In Nine Chapters or Less
by Anis Shivani

SHORT FICTION

Notes From the Mother Tongue
by An Tran

The Protester Has Been Released
by Janet Sarbanes

ESSAY AND CREATIVE NONFICTION

Immigration Essays
by Sybil Baker

Je suis l'autre: Essays and Interrogations
by Kristina Marie Darling

Death of Art
by Chris Campanioni

POETRY

Imagine Not Drowning
by Kelli Allen

Collected Lies and Love Poems
by John Reed

Tall as You are Tall Between Them
by Annie Christain

The Couple Who Fell to Earth
by Michelle Bitting

ANTHOLOGY

Zombies, Aliens, Cyborgs and the Ongoing Apocolypse
by Travis Denton and Katie Chaple

CHAPBOOKS

Notes from the Negro Side of the Moon
by Earl Braggs

A Hunger Called Music: A Verse History in Black Music
by Meredith Nnoka

cuntstruck
by Kate Northrop

Relief Map
by Erin M. Bertram

CPSIA information can be obtained
at www.ICGtesting.com
Printed in the USA
LVOW08s0013150317
527246LV00001B/151/P